The Emerging of the Nehemiahs

Copyright © 2023 by Kahlil White

ISBN: 978-1-7375082-3-6

All rights reserved. No part of this book may be reproduced, stored in a retrieval system, or transmitted in any form or by any means--electronic, mechanical, digital, photocopy, or any other without prior permission from the publisher and author, except as provided by the United States of America copyright law.

Unless otherwise noted, all scriptures are from the KING JAMES VERSION, public domain.

Scripture quotations marked (NIV) are taken from THE HOLY BIBLE, NEW INTERNATIONAL VERSION®. Copyright© 1973, 1978, 1984, 2011 by Biblica, Inc.™. Used by permission of Zondervan

Scripture quotations marked (NKJV) are taken from the NEW KING JAMES VERSION®. Copyright© 1982 by Thomas Nelson, Inc. Used by permission. All rights reserved.

Scripture quotations marked (NLT) are taken from the Holy Bible, New Living Translation, copyright ©1996, 2004, 2015 by Tyndale House Foundation. Used by permission of Tyndale House Publishers, Carol Stream, Illinois 60188. All rights reserved.

Scripture quotations marked (GNT) are from the Good News Translation in Today's English Version- Second Edition Copyright © 1992 by American Bible Society. Used by Permission.

Scripture quotations marked (NASB) are taken from the NEW AMERICAN STANDARD BIBLE®, Copyright© 1960, 1962, 1963, 1968, 1971, 1972, 1973, 1975, 1977, 1995 by The Lockman Foundation. Used by permission.

Scripture quotations marked (ESV) are taken from THE HOLY BIBLE, ENGLISH STANDARD VERSION®, Copyright© 2001 by Crossway, a publishing ministry of Good News Publishers. Used by permission.

Scripture quotations marked MSG are taken from THE MESSAGE, copyright © 1993, 2002, 2018 by Eugene H. Peterson. Used by permission of NavPress, represented by Tyndale House Publishers. All rights reserved.

Scripture quotations marked (Amp) are taken from the AMPLIFIED® BIBLE, Copyright© 1954, 1958, 1962, 1964, 1965, 1987 by the Lockman Foundation Used by Permission. (www.Lockman.org)

Scripture quotations marked (CEV) are taken from the CONTEMPORARY ENGLISH VERSION, Copyright© 1995 by the American Bible Society. Used by permission.

Scripture quotations marked TPT are from The Passion Translation®. Copyright © 2017, 2018, 2020 by Passion & Fire Ministries, Inc. Used by permission. All rights reserved. ThePassionTranslation.com.

Acknowledgements

Thank you to my mother, Sondra Wright, for her unwavering love and commitment throughout my life. Her support ensured that I, and the anointing on my life, was protected and that I had the necessary tools to walk in my purpose and fulfill my destiny with ease.

Thank you to my Pastor, Dr. R Shaun Ferguson, who has been an intricate part of my life and ministry. He has both pushed and provoked me into another level of purpose and faith. I would like to acknowledge Apostle Dannie & Dr. Precious Williams, who God did me a big favor when he connected me to them and the grace on their lives. Apostle Dannie Williams, as a seasoned Apostle, has pastored and helped me through some very dark and difficult moments and seasons and into some very victorious seasons and places in my life. He has also shared principles with me that has caused my gifts to become more potent.

To my mentor, Prophet Vince Williams, whom God has been kind enough to give me a seat at his table; ever since then the rivers of God have flowed out of me like never before. I have become a different

KIND and have gained more insight and understanding of the prophetic and the importance of purity for those who are prophetic.

To whom I refer to as my covenant-parents, Ministers Fabian & Makeya Tapper, I am deliciously grateful to God for my connection to them. These two have epitomized and represented soundness to and in my life.

Thank you to the entire BHFH family for helping this project come to life. And to the many supporters throughout my life, I am grateful for the part you all have played in helping me become who I am.

Table of Contents

Introduction..1
Repentance..15
No Time To Waste..23
Can God Trust You?...29
Arise & Build (Resistance & Retaliation)..43
Relationships...62
Walls, Gates, & Doors (Entrance & Exit Portals)............................67
He Will Prosper Us..77
7 Questions, 7 Answers..83
Solutions & Strategies..88
Audience..108
A Prevailing Spirit...113
5 Fold Gift...124
The Table..134
Ephesians 6:12...137
A Builder's Praise...144
Don't Fear...150
The Selfless Leader (Governmental Gatekeepers)..........................166
Two-Fold In The Assignment (Watch & Fight, Work & Build).......184
Refresh, Don't Relax...203
Sound..208
Crossover..223
The Forging Of Something New..227
A New Era: Revival..249
Checking The Records..268
What Judgment Against Blending Looks Like...............................279
The Dangerous Mentality..282
Sensitivity..285
Who's Guarding The Gates?..289
The Forcing Of An Agenda...291

The House Of God	*300*
The Sabbath	*305*
Kingdom Living	*308*
Functioning & Prospering In An Unfamiliar Place	*313*
If You Knew Everything	*320*
Dependency	*323*
Hanani	*331*
What To Expect Part 1 (Prophecy)	*338*
What To Expect Part 2 (Prophecy)	*340*
What To Expect Part 3 (Prophecy)	*342*
Type Of Christ	*346*
References	*348*

Introduction

What would make a man leave a place of comfort to go where there is definite calamity? Purpose! Purpose must have been important to Nehemiah. For one to pursue purpose, they must disappear from the place where they are to eventually appear in another. What is their appearing called? Emerging! There comes a point in every individual's life when their emergence is necessary. This will be the determining factor between whether one just exists on earth or lives the God-best life. When one just exists, they go through the rituals and routines of life without a true sense of purpose. When one lives a God-best life, they live and function the way that He intended them to. God's desire and design is for His children to reach the place that He has predestined and ordained them to walk in. The great thing about every person that emerges by the sovereignty and will of God is that it is either predestined or God foreknew it. In Jeremiah 1:5 (KJV), God tells Jeremiah, *"Before I formed thee in the belly I knew thee; and before thou camest forth out of the womb I sanctified thee, and I ordained thee a prophet unto the nations."* It is apparent from this statement that God knew Jeremiah in-eternity before he entered time and had already predestined him to live a certain life, function a certain way, and emerge in a certain era.

An emergence never happens by coincidence but by covenant. An example of God foreknowing of an emergence was David emerging as a leader. Though he wasn't God's first choice, Saul was, God still knew that it would happen. Dear reader, your emergence is necessary and predestined! I wholeheartedly believe that not emerging at the time God has ordained for one to emerge will cause that individual to be frustrated moving forward in their life. They'll be frustrated because they are not in the place where they have been called to function in. To emerge, however, one must first be hidden. Can you handle being hidden while understanding through revelation that you've been predestined to appear at a set time?

Years ago, during a moment of both mentoring and correction, Apostle Dannie Williams said to me, "Don't peak your pace; pace your peak." Meaning, don't rush or attempt to skip over the process you've been ordained to walk through to get to your destined place. He used the example of how it was God's will that David be King of Israel after King Saul's rebellion. However, David was processed and anointed two other times before being anointed the third time to be King of Israel. His initial anointing came in 1 Samuel 16:1 & 11-13, his second in 2 Samuel 2:1-4 to be King of Judah, and lastly in 2 Samuel 5:1-5 to be King over all of Israel and Judah. David would've been in trouble if he had tried to be King of Israel with the first anointing he received. Pace yourself and go through the necessary process that God will take you through to get to where He ultimately wants you to be.

In late 2020, I began to sense the Word of the Lord to write a book with Nehemiah's life as the focus and subject. I sensed that it was the Word of the Lord for this era. Nehemiah's emergence was important for him, his generation, and the time in which he existed. As it was in scripture, so it is today. Modern-day Nehemiahs have been and are emerging! Emerge comes from the Latin word emergere, which is made up of two parts, "E" and "mergere." (Harper, 2020) E is a variant of ex and it means out, and former. Mergere means to "dip or sink". Therefore, when one emerges, it is because God has moved them out of what is now a former place and into a new place. A place of purpose.

Nehemiahs have emerged and continue to do so with the grace and anointing on their lives to advance the Kingdom of God and bring transformation to a dying world. God is activating this remnant of people because their function is necessary to demonstrate heaven's agenda throughout the earth in this contemporary culture. It's not uncommon for Nehemiahs to be engaged in affairs that have captured their attention; however, deep down they know that they are called for more. They know there's more to life than where they currently are. Circumstances such as jobs, businesses, family affairs, and life issues have altered their course, and as a result, their life is in a place where God never called them to be. We see this in the life of Nehemiah, as he was born in captivity. He was the king's cupbearer, and even though being in this position was not his choice, it was his reality. The good news in this is that God uses every opportunity to bring glory to Himself and to advance His Kingdom; He does not waste experiences that one has encountered or walked through in life. It wasn't God's best that His people be taken captive, have their children be born in captivity, or even become exiled in the first place. However, because of their disobedience and that of their forefathers, He allowed it to happen. God, however, led them in paths of righteousness for His name's sake. This is because what God did for and through Nehemiah wasn't about Nehemiah but about and for His divine purpose. That is why the calling of God on one's life should always keep them humbled because He is allowing them to partner with Him. Nehemiah's emergence represented restoration for the people and the place he was called to. Only God can restore one man and use that man's restoration to provoke a ripple effect for one, thousands, hundreds of thousands, millions, and billions of people. Therefore, it is imperative that one understands that their surrendering and submission to God is critical. One's submission to God isn't just beneficial to them but to those who are connected and assigned to their life and voice. Nehemiah's restoration triggered the restoration of many other lives by God's divine power. The word restoration in Greek is the word "apokathistémi," and it means "to restore, or give back". (Biblehub.com) The usage of apokathistémi points to reinstating someone or something to its original position or condition. The first part of the word "apokathistémi" is the Greek word "apo" and means "away from". The second part of the word is the Greek word "kathistémi" and means "to set in order", or "to appoint". In this restoration of Nehemiah's life, God had to apo him. God had to take him away from the place where he was in the palace at Shushan and free his hands of what had him occupied. The place where he was had become too small for him. It was time for Nehemiah to function and operate in what God had placed on his life. That, however, couldn't be done at the palace at Shushan in the capacity and at the level that God intended. Isaiah 49:20 (GNT) says, *"Your people who were born in exile will one day say to you, 'This land is too small - we need more room to live in!"* Live also means to function. The Israelites who returned from captivity knew they needed more room to live. I believe that Nehemiah knew he had greatness in him. However, he may have never known the full extent of it had he not moved out of the palace at Shushan. He had to be placed in an environment where he had room to fully function as who he truly was. The full manifestation of his greatness wasn't seen and didn't come out of him until he came to the land of Judah and Jerusalem. What if Nehemiah would have gotten frustrated in Persia and said, "I know I'm anointed to do more, but these people in Persia don't recognize it." He would have been trying to gain an audience with people that he wasn't called to minister to in a certain capacity. One of the worst things an anointed person can do is expect acceptance and recognition in every place and in every season of their life. It opens the door for the spirit of rejection to operate because of how badly they want to be accepted. After God "apoed" and moved him away from the palace at Shushan, he could then experience the second part of restoration for his life, the "kathistémi." Now that his hands were free of his job, he could be appointed to the place God had ordained, which will be discussed throughout this book. Nehemiah's life had some twists and turns, but he still ended up right where God wanted him to be. He still found the place of his assignment. God is a master at shifting courses and pulling people into their assignments despite the odds. Nehemiah acquired information about the Jews who had escaped captivity, those who were left in captivity, and the state of Jerusalem. Upon receiving this information, he was moved with grief. You can truly begin to discover your calling when you are moved with compassion concerning a particular thing. Nehemiah knew in his heart that he had to take action with the information that he received concerning Jerusalem. At this point, we see God begin to awaken this mighty man of valor, though he knew all along he was anointed to do more. As you are reading this, I want you to know that you are anointed for more. After Nehemiah became aware of his assignment, God began using him to fulfill the task that he was called to do.

Emerging Nehemiahs are those who are called to build and shift economies. An economy is the wealth and resources of a country or region, especially in terms of the production and consumption of goods and services. (Wikipedia, 2022) God uses His prophets to speak, shift, and preserve economies. Elisha the prophet was used by God to prophesy and speak to the economy of Samaria, and it transpired within 24 hours in 2 Kings 7:1. God used Joseph to release wisdom that caused the economy of Egypt to be preserved during a famine. God will use the emergence of Nehemiahs to cause a great resurgence in economies. This will further open the door for believers to testify about Jesus Christ and His supernatural power. As God does a new thing by using His chosen vessels to build and rebuild economies, we will see reverence and honor for God, His work, and vessels in the earth. This remnant is called to build, and as they do, we will see them rise above obstacles and challenges that will be present and persistent as they endeavor to fulfill their purpose and Kingdom assignment. Whenever builders appear, they represent birthing and manifestation. What God has done in heaven: He sends a builder to birth in the earth.

In the natural world, builders and construction workers only show up to a construction site after being permitted to by someone who has the authority. Their green light to appear at the construction site to build comes after management has negotiated details, received payment, and has the blueprint of the property. Therefore, when God allows builders to emerge, it's because He has settled what He wants to do in the earth. God has been using His servants, the builders, since the beginning of time as instruments of destiny to do and fulfill His plans and purposes. We see it throughout the Bible, mostly in the Old

Testament. The builder's anointing is powerful because it enables man to divinely construct what is necessary for the Kingdom of God, governments, systems, others, themselves, and their seed. Cain, Moses, Zerubbabel, King David, King Solomon, the young prophets whom Elisha the prophet mentored, Uzziah, and King Hezekiah all were builders, and these are just a few of the many people in the Bible who were. Emerging Nehemiahs will lead nations and armies into purpose. Other builders will be birthed because of the word and aura that Nehemiahs exude. The beginning of Isaiah 41:7 (KJV), *"So the carpenter encouraged the goldsmith...,"* teaches us that builders encourage and push other builders into purpose. Emerging Nehemiahs will also carry the spirit of innovation regarding technology. Technology is the invention of useful things that have provided solutions to so many problems. In Exodus 31:1-6, we see how God anointed individuals to develop technology.

Exodus 31:1-6 (KJV)

1. And the Lord spake unto Moses, saying,

2. See, I have called by name Bezaleel the son of Uri, the son of Hur, of the tribe of Judah:

3. And I have filled him with the spirit of God, in wisdom, and in understanding, and in knowledge, and in all manner of workmanship,

4. To devise cunning works, to work in gold, and in silver, and in brass,

5. And in cutting of stones, to set them, and in carving of timber, to work in all manner of workmanship.

6. And I, behold, I have given with him Aholiab, the son of Ahisamach, of the tribe of Dan: and in the hearts of all that are wise hearted I have put wisdom, that they may make all that I have commanded thee.

As the Lord called Bezaleel and filled him with His Spirit, wisdom, understanding, and knowledge, so too He called Aholiab to invent, create, and build. They built what was vital to the children of Israel's history for generations to come and are types, shadows, and symbols in this current time. Many people have questions and problems, wondering what's next while navigating through difficult times. The good news is that the answer will be hidden and cultivated within God's chosen vessels. Nehemiahs will create and build what the world is looking for and needs.

A great move of God is currently hitting the earth in this new era and age, and the next generation of generals in the faith will be awakened and utilized. They will appear, and people will wonder where they came from as they bring about great change. This next move of God will not be limited to just ministry within the confines of the church but will touch every mountain, system, part of the world, and individuals' lives. Often, when people see and sense a move of God, they quickly attempt to box it in and limit it to just church when God desires to do much more, but this current shift has already begun. It will shake every system. This is a peculiar era in which God is using peculiar people to do peculiar exploits. This generation in which the hand of the Lord is upon will be very different. They will do things outside the box but still within the Bible. In the book of Luke, Jesus healed a paralyzed man brought to him on a couch by his friends. The Bible says in Luke 5:26 (KJV), *"And they were all amazed, and they glorified God, and were filled with fear, saying, We have seen strange things to day."* Lexico.com defines peculiar as odd or unusual. People will be amazed at what God does through this generation. It will then lead them to give glory to God. It will cause people to have a deep and reverential fear for the Lord. People will then acknowledge that they have seen strange things that are unusual and different from what they expected to see.

As we look at David's life in scripture, we see the early stages of his emergence and entrance to the public scene as he defeats Goliath. It's important to understand how significant the beginning of David's emergence is, because when David defeated Goliath, Israel was saved. It brought salvation and deliverance to a people and an entire country. This victory was powerful and significant because David won a battle that his brothers were already fighting. There is a remnant emerging that will conquer and defeat what others have been contending with but haven't been able to get victory over. We see in scripture that Saul offered his equipment to David when he was ready to war against Goliath and the Philistines. This represents a constant trend of people thinking that you can't do a task unless you do it in a particular way. Still, the anointing will defy what the intellectuals are accustomed to and what small-minded individuals are limited to comprehending. David respectfully turned down Saul's equipment because he knew that he had his own grace, and it was unlike anything Israel had ever seen before. David represents a new era, and dispensation. In the emergence of Nehemiahs, this next move of God will be unlike anything we've ever seen, and it won't be limited and confined.

Nehemiah's name means "consolation", and "repentance of the Lord". (Hitchcock, 1869) Consolation means "the comfort received by a person after the loss or disappointment". When Nehemiah arrived in Judah, he helped those assigned to his life live better lives and fulfill God's will for their lives. Nehemiahs are arising and emerging as a consolation of hope for many individuals. People all over the world have had missteps and mishaps, and because of this, they have quit on their purpose. Nehemiahs are, however, coming to cancel disappointments through words of life that they will release over lives and into situations. One of the assignments of these leaders will be to help people take their disappointments and use them as fuel to get back in the race, run it, and get everything that God has for them. People will trust emerging Nehemiahs because of the authenticity of their voice and genuine nature. The Kingdom of God is within believers, and we've been called to affect and bring impact to the seven mountains of influence. The seven mountains of influence are religion, family, education, government, media, entertainment, and business (Ezekiel 36:1).

Emerging Nehemiahs will produce in every mountain because of who they represent and what they carry on their life.

While you are reading this, can I prophesy to you? Get up, man of God! Get up, woman of God! You will not die but live and declare the works of Almighty God! Every disappointment is being turned into purpose. This isn't your end; God is giving you another wind and grace to run your race.

Repentance

Nehemiah's initial response after receiving the information concerning the Jews who had escaped, the state of Jerusalem, and people who were left in captivity, was repentance. He repented of 3 different groups of sins.

Nehemiah 1:6 (KJV) – "Let thine ear now be attentive, and thine eyes open, that thou mayest hear the prayer of thy servant, which I pray before thee now, day and night, for the children of Israel thy servants, and confess the sins of the children of Israel, which we have sinned against thee: both I and my father's house have sinned."

1. Personal Sins ("…both I…")

2. Generational Sins ("…my father's house…")

3. National Sins ("…confess the sins of the children of Israel…")

It is very important to understand what repentance does. It reverses what was destined to transpire because of a spiritual law that has been set in motion through one's words or actions. We are living in a time where repentance is needed to truly reverse outcomes that have come between God's people and their fulfillment. The word repent was used by the Greek military as a command to, "about-face" or turn around to face the opposite direction. Before the glory of God can be seen, God's people must about-face. This is why living a repentant life is vital because it keeps you conscious of anything that would separate you from God and His plans for your life.

1. Personal Sins: **(both I)** Nehemiah's prayer of repentance was one of understanding. He knew he couldn't effectively walk in his assignment from God with unrepented sin in his life. Sin halts and shuts down what God wants to do in a person's life in any capacity.

2. Generational Sins: **(my father's house)** It matters not who specifically committed the sin or sins; if that sin or those sins have opened a door creating generational cycles, curses, and bondages and are preventing God from moving, then they need to be repented of. Nehemiah was closing a door when he said, "we have sinned." He was going back to the root of where the sin began. It is important to take ownership of hindrance that has been transferred generationally. If a previous generation was righteous and followed God with all their heart, resulting in God honoring the next generation, they would gladly receive and take ownership of what God is releasing to them. If people respond

to generational blessings by receiving them, then they must be just as intentional in how they respond to generational curses. These generational curses can't be ignored but should be acknowledged to be reversed and canceled.

3. Nations: **(confess the sins of the children of Israel)** Nations must and need to repent in order to see the hand of God move there. What a nation sees in the natural is an indication of what is happening in the spirit. There are events that occur because that nation as a whole has sinned. Joshua knew that God's people should have walked in victory the first time they confronted Ai, but instead, they were defeated. The Lord had to reveal to Joshua that Israel had sinned, and this was the reason why they didn't see victory. Sin can completely shut down your assignment from God. After Joshua discovered that Achan was the reason Israel wasn't walking in victory, Achan was killed because he took of the accursed things. As Achan was killed, we must always kill what will cost us victory. Achan's story is indicative of the reality that man must always disassociate themselves from what can contaminate them. The Bible is clear in 2 Chronicles 7:14 (KJV) that *"If my people, which are called by my name, shall humble themselves, and pray, and seek my face, and turn from their wicked ways; then will I hear from heaven, and will forgive their sin, and*

will heal their land." This gives in-depth details of what happens when people repent. It leads to reversal. During the time of Nehemiah's repentance, the land of Jerusalem and Judah needed healing, and we see the hand of the Lord move to heal the land after Nehemiah's cry of repentance.

Nehemiah praying for the nations also showed that he was a national leader. His prayer wasn't focused only on himself but also on others. He was praying for who he felt called to. Therefore, if you feel called to the nations, you must pray for the nations you feel called to. If you feel called to a region, then you must pray for the region you feel called to.

Nehemiah 1:8-9 (KJV) – "Remember, I beseech thee, the word that thou commandest thy servant Moses, saying, If ye transgress, I will scatter you abroad among the nations: But if ye turn unto me, and keep my commandments, and do them; though there were of you cast out unto the uttermost part of the heaven, yet will I gather them from thence, and will bring them unto the place that I have chosen to set my name there."

Disobedience has caused men to be moved from the post and position that they were ordained to hold. When the Bible alludes to the children of Israel being scattered abroad in the Old Testament, it means that they got moved from their destined place because of their rebellion against God. The Lord did not want to evict Adam and Eve from the garden of Eden. Adam and Eve signed their own eviction notice with the pen of disobedience, which houses the ink of death. God always intends for His people to be in a place of purification and sanctification. God is gathering those whose repentance is real and is allowing them to walk in their purpose. We will also see an emerging of those who've gone off track because of disobedience and rebellion against God, but whose heart God has gotten a hold of. These people must know that they have not missed their purpose, because as long as there is still breath in their body, then there is still time to walk in their purpose.

Nehemiah 1:11 (KJV) – *"O Lord, I beseech thee, let now thine ear be attentive to the prayer of thy servant, and to the prayer of thy servants, who desire to fear thy name: and prosper, I pray thee, thy servant this day, and grant him mercy in the sight of this man. For I was the king's cupbearer."*

(Who desire to fear thy name…)

Nehemiah, in his prayer of repentance, confessed that he and the rest of God's people desired to fear the name of God, which means to have a reverential fear for God and the things of God. He was praying for what was needed in that particular hour and is likewise needed in this current era of emerging Nehemiahs. The day has arrived where God is doing a great work in the lives of his people, the church, and in the earth. As a result of this, there has returned a reverential fear for God and the things of God. Reverence and respect are the doors that lead to honor. Therefore, now that honor for God and His Kingdom has returned, it will create environments and atmospheres for God to manifest Himself, even amongst those who haven't given their life to Jesus Christ.

Repentance to God without reverence for God is simply temporary physiological appeasement with hopes of receiving something from God. However, without a true commitment internally to change and external application, it makes that repentance false. I've often heard older generations say there was a time when even those who weren't saved had such respect for God. So much so that when people would pass by a church, they would turn down ungodly music, stop using profanity, and stop doing anything else deemed disrespectful towards God.

(And prosper…)

Nehemiah in his prayer of repentance said that he and the rest of God's people desired to prosper. Why would Nehemiah mention prospering in his prayer of repentance? It's because a lack of repentance can and will affect the prosperity of a person and or people. Nehemiah was praying this on behalf of people who were, at that time, a reproach to other nations. They were living in a dilapidated economy that was not thriving. When there is a lack of repentance, it will halt movement. God is showing His people what is hindering the progress in their lives and exposing what is obstructing them from fulfilling His will in the earth. Nehemiah praying this represented God's heart for movement.

Emerging Nehemiahs will be the voices that pray the mind of God concerning what's hindering progress so that heaven can be seen on earth. This is the reason why prayer must never be approached casually but critically. Nehemiah stood as an intercessor for a nation he wasn't physically in at that moment, but his intercession shifted an entire nation. God uses His intercessors to pray and intercede for nations and regions that they may have never been. What an honor this was for Nehemiah and is for those whom the Lord uses to do His work.

Let's pray this prayer together, "Lord, I submit to you. Use me to prophetically pray what's on your mind, always, that will shift the trajectory of the place that you've given me a burden and passion for in Jesus' name, Amen."

God wants His people to prosper and advance. When Jesus began His ministry, He made a statement in Matthew 4:17, *"Repent: for the kingdom of heaven is at hand."* Jesus, in making this statement, was urging those listening to change your way of thinking and living, because a Kingdom has arrived on earth that you can be a part of, and it is constantly moving and advancing.

No Time To Waste

Nehemiah 2:6 (KJV) – "Then the king said to me, with the queen sitting beside him, "How long will your journey be, and when will you return?" So it pleased the king to send me, and I gave him a definite time."

The King asked Nehemiah two questions.

1. How long shall thy journey be?

2. When will thou return?

The king's relationship with Nehemiah is a type of relationship between God and His children. After the king asked Nehemiah these questions, and he answered them, then the king was pleased to send him. Nehemiah informed both the king and queen how long his journey would be. Giving them a set time when he would return is symbolic of the reality that time is of the essence. Emerging Nehemiahs don't have the luxury of wasting time because the Body of Christ is in an era where we can't afford to miss God. Long gone are the days when one was able to spend time procrastinating, recovering from intentional decisions that weren't God's best, and wasting energy on what has nothing to do with Kingdom purpose and assignment. One bad decision can take years to recover from. Just imagine if Nehemiah would have gotten distracted from his assignment during the time the king sent him out and started making decisions that weren't God's best for his life. When it would have been time to return to the king, he would have either missed his entire assignment that he was sent out to do or been in the middle of trying to recover from decisions that he made. Prophet Vince Williams has said for many years that "It is better to avoid a thing than to have to recover from it." Just because God can redeem the time doesn't mean it's a license to waste it. Nehemiah only had a season to complete the work that he was sent out to do, and had he missed that, he would have missed God. This is why it's important to maximize seasons, opportunities, and moments that God gives to you. We, as believers, can't have the mindset that if I miss God in this season, I'll obey Him and do what He wants me to do in the next season. You may never step into a season like that again. It's all according to God's sovereignty. Some moments only come once in a lifetime, and if missed, won't come back around for many years. These moments that I'm speaking of are what I call God-moments, which are supernatural and divine and are used by God to shift the entire trajectory of your life. Elisha had a once-in-a-lifetime experience when he received the mantle from Elijah. I believe that had he missed that moment, he may have never experienced another like it.

As Nehemiah in his time did what he was assigned to do quickly, so must emerging Nehemiahs. These are seasons when the enemy will send the most distractions because he knows what it will cost the one who becomes consumed by the distractions he sends. He will do whatever he can to halt what God wants to do through a person. People tend to focus only on the forgiveness of God, which is great, but this is only half of the story. Will God forgive a man for intentional sins and for him making decisions that aren't his best or will for his life? He absolutely will! 1 John 1:9 (KJV) teaches that *"If we confess our sins, he is faithful and just to forgive us our sins, and to cleanse us from all unrighteousness."* Everyone gets excited over the fact that God will forgive them of their sins, as they should. What a blessing it is to know that when we fall short of the glory of God, He will forgive us. People, however, often fail to realize that though God forgives, it does not negate the reality of consequences for the sin that they've committed. The issue comes when one must recover from their sinful, unwise decision and then be faced with the possibility they forfeited what God wanted to do through, with, or for them that they may never see again. Moments and seasons are crucial, and every one of them must be approached with extreme caution. Also, some moments and seasons require that you not only to be obedient but also to move expeditiously in and through them because of the current demand. Judas experienced this kind of moment when Jesus told him in John 13:7 (ESV): *"What you are going to do, do quickly."* Jesus saying this to Judas, to do whatever he's going to do quickly, was Him embracing the will of God according to Psalms 41:9 (NKJV). Psalm 41:9 says, *"Yea, mine own familiar friend, in whom I trusted, which did eat of my bread, hath lifted up his heel against me."* It was also significant of the importance of doing some things quickly. Jesus couldn't be crucified until Judas betrayed Him, so He had to tell Judas to do what prophecy said he would do. Judas didn't have any time to waste. Therefore, he had to be focused on quickly betraying Jesus; even though it wasn't beneficial for Judas, the prophecy had to be fulfilled.

Your focus determines your finale. The story of Judas represented Jesus being willing to partner with prophecy, no matter how it would make him feel in that moment. We are in an era where people must be willing to do whatever it takes to see the manifestation of prophecies spoken over their lives. It doesn't matter how bad things may currently look in their lives. Put a demand on the prophecy spoken over your life by warring with it and submitting to God's perfect will to see it come to pass. There is no time to waste when one has a prophecy over their life. Jesus had many prophecies over His life, which is why He conducted the Last Supper as He did. The Last Supper wasn't just a meal; it was a moment. A moment that had a demand on it. Jesus making His statement to Judas was tantamount to Him telling Judas to "Sell me for 30 pieces of silver, which will lead to me being beaten and humiliated. This will ultimately lead to me being afflicted, suffering, and crucified on the cross." When one's heart is settled on ministry, a moment of suffering won't stop them. That's why Jesus was able to ask for what would lead to His suffering. If not wasting time or not missing a moment meant that you had to embrace suffering, affliction, and resistance, could you do it? Jesus had to be apostolic even while being afflicted because a part of being apostolic is the trials and suffering that come along with it. Jesus could've said, "If Judas does what prophecy says that he's supposed to do, it's going to inconvenience Me, so I'm not going to tell him." No, Jesus didn't do this. He embraced the moment and understood the obedience that was demanded of Him in that particular moment. As Philippians 2:8 (KJV) says, *"he humbled himself, and became obedient unto death, even the death of the cross. As a result of his obedience the entire plan of salvation everyone who will accept it."*

Can God Trust You?

Nehemiah 2:4 (KJV) – "Then the king said unto me, For what dost thou make request? So I prayed to the God of heaven."

Nehemiah was presented with a God-given opportunity but didn't use it to push his own agenda. This is because he could be trusted. God is moving away from those who for so long have pushed their own agendas for their own gain, through doors that He's opened for them to build His Kingdom.

During a phone conversation with Apostle Dannie L. Williams in late September of 2021, he said, "Kahlil, the question now is not whether or not you trust God. The question now is, Can God trust you?" God is opening doors and presenting opportunities strictly for Kingdom advancement. The king asked Nehemiah what his request was. This was a God moment that was presented to Nehemiah. Nehemiah modeled in this moment how God expects His children and those who He trusts to steward God moments. He prayed and sought the face of God as to what he should do with such a great opportunity. After Nehemiah expressed his heart, which was God's heart, and told his vision, there came provision for the journey he was about to go on. This is why God plants His people in places of authority in the earth to express His heart and will in the earth. God is giving great provision to those He can trust to carry out the vision He has given to them. Believers also have the right to ask God for provision for the assignment that He's given to them. The Apostle, in writing to the church at Philippi in Philippians 4:6 (KJV), said, *"Be careful for nothing; but in every thing by prayer and supplication with thanksgiving let your requests be made known unto God."* Therefore, as Nehemiah made his request to the king, it is symbolic of the reality that believers can make their request to God. Some people lack provision the way God desires them to have it because their own agendas are more important to them than God's agenda. We are living in an hour where Kingdom ambassadors must be prayerful about everything as the Lord releases God-moments to advance the Kingdom. Many have taken God's moments and used them to advance their own lives because of impure motives. The Lord is, however, now looking for a remnant that He can trust with what He wants to birth in the earth. In Acts 6:1-8 the Grecians were murmuring against the Hebrews because they felt their widows were being neglected. The Apostles at this time had such a high demand on them for ministry and couldn't attend to everything. Acts 6:3 (KJV) says, *"Wherefore, brethren, look ye out among you seven men of honest report, full of the Holy Ghost and wisdom, whom we may appoint over this business."* This is what the Lord is doing and now. He's looking for those who are honest with pure motives so that as He presents opportunities for Kingdom advancement, they won't use it to promote their personal agenda. God is raising up Spirit-filled individuals whom He can trust not to compromise. This remnant will walk in great wisdom and know what to do when God presents opportunities. They will know the mind of God and the movements of God because of their prayer life. These are the people who the Lord is appointing, raising up, causing to emerge, and putting on the hearts of leaders in the Body of Christ. Those leaders will pour into and help this remnant get to the next level. This is the prelude to the Stephens who are coming on the scene, who are servants and don't necessarily hold five-fold offices or high positions but walk in great power and authority.

Prophet Vince Williams once said during a message he was preaching that "God is more interested in inspection than rewarding, and based on what He sees in your heart, it will affect what He trusts to release into your hand." In addition to this statement, Prophet Vince Williams also once said, "When your heart is proven, then you have nothing to prove." It is God who proves man's heart to be pure.

Nehemiah's heart had been proven by God, and that's why God allowed him to come into the opportunity that he came into with the king in Nehemiah 2. Nehemiah did not show up to the place of his assignment with a chip on his shoulder, trying to prove what he was called to do to anyone. He showed up and functioned! This is because Nehemiah knew that he had nothing to prove.

God can trust a person who knows they don't have anything to prove to people. When one has something to prove, they'll make ministry about themselves because they feel inadequate. The Bible says in Luke 12:48 (KJV), "For unto whomsoever much is given, of him shall be much required." When the King asked Nehemiah in Nehemiah 2:4 (NKJV), "What do you request?", much was being given to Nehemiah. Nehemiah, in response, did what was required of him, which was seek God for direction because of the offer given to him by the king. The latter part of Luke 12:48 in the International Standard Version says, "But even more will be demanded from the one to whom much has been entrusted." Nehemiah was entrusted with so much from the Lord, and with that came a great demand for what was on his life. Whenever there is a great demand, there must be a greater dedication to uphold the standard of God. The Lord could not have placed someone in the position Nehemiah held who was not trustworthy. God's people were in a vulnerable position due to what they were experiencing. Therefore, when Nehemiah showed up to the place of his assignment with everything that was on his life, there was a great demand for him to function and give his life over to the work of God. This is why private development is imperative. When one allows God to process them in private, they'll be spiritually mature enough to handle public ministry and the demand that comes with it. Now, it's important to know that what manifests through a person in public is an indication of what has or hasn't been developed in them in private. Just think, Nehemiah immediately went from being in the king's shadow to leading an entire nation once he experienced a God-moment. That took maturity. I'm sure Nehemiah felt the pressure of his assignment and all that came along with it. One moment he's serving at the palace of Shushan, and the next he's serving an entire nation and combating darkness to defend against Sanballat, Tobiah, Geshem, and the rest of his enemies. God must know that He can trust you before your moment comes. Nehemiah was processed and, as a result, prepared, and when pressure came, he didn't fold but stood firm. He also suddenly had access to wealth (materials) to build the wall and governed the wealth of the nation of

Judah. He never abused the power that he had, nor did he mishandle the wealth that he had access to. When you give a person access to certain tools, such as wealth and power, it usually provides the opportunity to see who they really are. Nehemiah's ability to responsibly handle power and wealth shows us why God could trust him.

Nehemiah, as the king's cupbearer, risked his life daily for the king, which means that he was willing to die for the one he was serving. This door for Nehemiah would possibly never have opened had he not been in a place of serving and being willing to die for the one he was serving. Jesus said in Matthew 10:39 (KJV), *"He that findeth his life shall lose it: and he that loseth his life for my sake shall find it."* Nehemiah was willing to lose his life for the king's sake. He tasted his food and drink before the king, and because he did, he found God's best and stepped into his God-assignment. When Jesus said, *"he that findeth his life, shall lose it,"* He was talking about the one who follows his own way and plan verses God's. When one follows their own way and plans, they lose out on what God has for them but the one who gives up his life for God shall find the best life in God through Christ Jesus. When a man is willing to and gives up dreams and plans for God, God can then trust them. The reason being is because he is at least willing in his heart to submit to the God that he is serving. When God trusts a man, He not only brags on them (Job 1:8, Job 2:3), He also gives them what they desire because He knows He can trust them to be a good steward over it. I believe that when the king asked Nehemiah what his request was, he knew he was going to grant it to him because he knew that Nehemiah could be trusted with whatever he was about to ask for. This is a prophetic paradigm: the more God can trust you, the more he will open doors and give opportunities to you. There was a special relationship between Nehemiah and the king. We see this through how the king cared about Nehemiah's sadness in his presence. The king knew who he was granting the opportunity to. He knew the kind of person Nehemiah was. The king had a chance while Nehemiah was serving him to gauge his character, integrity, and how he conducted himself. This is one of the reasons it's important to have a relationship with the Lord because as we are trusting, serving, and giving our lives to Him and the work of His ministry, He's watching. As God watches us, He also processes us, after which He then knows that He can trust us more. One must also conduct themselves with character and integrity even in moments and seasons such as these because God is always watching. Every season has value to it, and every moment is critical, as one moment can shift one's life into the direction that God ordained for them to walk in. Ecclesiastes 11:6 (NIV) says, *"Sow your seed in the morning, and at evening let your hands not be idle, for you do not know which will succeed, whether this or that, or whether both will do equally well."* The one who is consistent, no matter the time or season, is the one whom God can trust.

I feel this while I'm writing this book. Prophesy over your life, reader, that "I'm one faithful decision away from seeing the harvest of the seed that I've sown." While we don't serve God solely to get blessings from Him, a part of our rights and privileges as believers in Christ Jesus is prosperity and possessing God's best. Believers should strive to have the kind of heart that the Apostle Peter had. The Apostle Peter told Jesus in Luke 22:32 (KJV), *"Lord, I am ready to go with thee, both into prison, and to death."* He said this to Jesus after Jesus gave him a prophetic word about the enemy desiring to sift him, but Jesus prayed for him. God's faithfulness to the Apostle Peter provoked the response of giving his all to God. That's when God knows that He can trust a man. When His blessings drive your heart closer to Him and your desire intensifies to give more of yourself to Him. Even though Jesus followed what the Apostle Peter said with telling Him that he would deny Him three times, He still trusted him. The reason being is because He already knew what would happen. Jesus trusted the Apostle Peter so much that there were some places that He only took him, along with the apostles James and John. The Apostle Peter experienced the shekinah glory of God, the voice of God, and supernatural visitation from Elijah and Moses on the Mount of Transfiguration along with the Apostles James and John. Jesus charged the three Apostles not to tell anyone, including the nine other apostles, what they experienced until a certain time. Those who the Lord can trust will experience Matthew 17:1-9 in the days to come.

1. (The Apostles Seen The Glory Of God) Matthew 17:5 (KJV), *"While he yet spake, behold, a bright cloud overshadowed them."*

Peter, James, and John saw the glory of God with their physical eyes. They were taken higher and deeper into the presence of God and experienced the glory of God that could not just be felt but seen. It's amazing how powerful God is. Only He can take a person deeper and higher at the same time. The glory of God is an eternal reality that comes out of one dimension and invades another. Therefore, those whom the Lord trusts will access, step into, and live in greater and higher dimensions because of the glory that they not only have access to but also carry. The Apostle Peter experienced the glory of God in Matthew 17, but from the book of Acts on throughout the New Testament, he carried it. Everything that man needs is in the glory of God. Throughout the Old Testament, whenever the glory of God appeared, it satisfied man to a level where he didn't need or desire anything else. God not only wants man to access another dimension, but He also wants man to live in another dimension, the realm in eternity where revelation is. The importance of man having this access is that he is able to access revelation out of an eternal realm and bring it into the lower realm on earth. This is also important because God doesn't want man to struggle to receive revelation. As man carries the glory that they've experienced, they will demonstrate the supernatural in spirit and power in the earth. Man experiences God in private, at which time deposits are made by God into man. He then demonstrates in public based on the level of what he's experienced in private.

2. (The Apostles Heard The Voice Of God) Matthew 17:5 (KJV), *"and behold a voice out of the cloud, which said, This is my beloved Son, in whom I am well pleased; hear ye him."*

Peter, James, and John heard the voice of the Father speaking from heaven. Their hearing increased and, they were privy to what the Father was saying. Those who the Lord trusts, He will allow to hear the intimate things that He's releasing at a greater level.

3. (The Apostles Seen A Vision, And Saw Jesus Experience A Divinely Granted Appointed Visitation) Matthew 17:3 (KJV), *"And, behold, there appeared unto them Moses and Elias…"*

Peter, James, and John saw Moses and Elias appear in a visitation and talk with Jesus. As the Spirit wills, those who the Lord trusts will experience supernatural visitations from the Lord through angels and in other ways that are in alignment with the word of God.

4. The Apostles Tapped Into Heaven Through Moses & Elias) Matthew 17:3 (KJV*),* *"…talking with him…"*

Peter, James, and John heard Moses and Elias talking with Jesus. What would the two prophets be talking to Jesus Christ about? The bible doesn't give insight into this conversation that Jesus had with Moses and Elias after Peter, James, and John came off the mountain. Jesus did give them revelation concerning what was happening in their era. The revelation was, that John the Baptist was carrying the spirit of Elias. They became aware of heaven's agendas. Being tapped into heaven is different from someone hearing God directly speak to them. This is where one is aware of what is happening in the spirit realm and the conversations that God has in heaven. In my own personal journey with the Lord, He has allowed me to have supernatural encounters where I'm in a place in the Spirit, and as I'm there, I can hear what God is saying from His throne room. In these encounters, He hasn't been talking to me directly, or about me, but I heard what was being released from heaven and what was being discussed in the counsel of the Lord. The Apostle Paul in 2 Corinthians 12:2-4 described an out-of-body experience that he had where he heard words that weren't lawful for him to utter in the earth. It doesn't say God spoke these words directly to the Apostle Paul, though it's possible. It states that the Apostle ascended into a higher dimension, the third heaven, and he started hearing discussions in heaven.

Through the Holy Spirit, those whom God trusts will access greater revelation, heaven's agenda, what's happening, and what's to come in their current era. Now, imagine how much Jesus had to trust the Apostle Peter to take him up to the Mount of Transfiguration, allow him to have that experience, and then challenge him not to tell anyone.

The Apostle Peter was the outspoken one amongst the 12 apostles and had quick responses to a lot that Jesus said. The one who was known for talking was the one God challenged to be silent about what was very tempting to share. This was a part of the Apostle Peter's development because God had to be able to trust him to keep that moment a secret until the appointed time. Nehemiah exhibits this in Nehemiah 2:12 when he inspected the land that he was getting ready to build in. It says, *"And I arose in the night, I and a few men with me; neither told I any man what my God had put in my heart to do at Jerusalem: neither was there any beast with me, save the beast that I rode upon."* Nehemiah waited until it was time for him to release what God put in his heart; therefore, he was trustworthy to handle much responsibility. In Luke 8, Jesus only took the apostles Peter, James, and John with him into Jairus's house. Why did He do this? I believe it was because He could trust these three to handle this intense moment in which somebody was dead. Jesus taking the Apostles into this moment also represented God opening doors and providing greater opportunities of ministry because He could trust them. There were many times when all 12 apostles were involved in ministry, but this moment in Jairus's house represented a new Kingdom platform that was available. The body of Christ is in a time when emerging Nehemiahs and all whom the Lord trusts will be exposed to greater opportunities of ministry. They will access platforms that they have been prepared for. This moment at Jairus's house is one the Apostle Peter needed to experience, as the Lord was trusting him with more. When the Lord trusts you, He will bring you before what He will eventually bring you into. The people at Jairus's house were laughing at Jesus's words even though He was 100% God, 100% man. He lived a supernatural life in which He demonstrated signs, wonders, miracles, and healing. With all the work he would do in the Kingdom, Peter needed to witness this so he would know how to handle all that he would eventually do in and for the Kingdom. He preached the first sermon of the church on the day of Pentecost. Peter also preached to the Gentiles, causing people other than Jews to receive the Holy Ghost in Acts 10, and wrote a portion of the New Testament. Therefore, evidence that God can trust you is that He takes you into places spiritually where you'll experience deeper and places physically that you've never been that only He can take you to experience greater.

Arise & Build (Resistance & Retaliation)

Nehemiah 2:18 (KJV) – "Then I told them of the hand of my God which was good upon me; as also the king's words that he had spoken unto me. And they said, Let us rise up and build. So they strengthened their hands for this good work."

Joshua 1:3 (KJV) says, *"Every place that the sole of your foot will tread upon I have given you, as I said to Moses."* God will never send you into territory that He has not already assigned to you. God will never send you on an apostolic assignment that He has not given you the victory and grace to take hold of. Therefore, go forth with the grace of a wise master builder and build (1 Corinthians 3:10). This remnant that's emerging in this contemporary culture will be wise master builders. They will possess great intelligence propelling them to build with excellence. Master builder is defined in Greek as "architektón" which is where the English word architect comes from, which means "someone responsible from the beginning to the end for the success (beauty, solidarity) of a building.]." (Biblehub.com) Emerging Nehemiahs will have a great responsibility in building whatever they've been assigned because to whom much is given, much is required. Architektón is made of two Greek words and has different functions. "Archó" means "to rule", "to begin", and "tektón" means "a craftsman, a carpenter." A wise master builder is one who designs the details of the framework of what they are building. It is also one who is highly skilled in their craft. Nehemiahs will be constructors who are hands-on in building. The work ethic of emerging Nehemiahs will be filled with energy, engagement, and enthusiasm while producing evidence. A great work ethic is important when doing God's work, as a poor work ethic with no consistent drive can hinder what God wants to do through an individual. Skillsets will also be important in the last days because they will make individuals more effective in a world that is shifting, changing, and transitioning in many ways. Emerging Nehemiahs will labor in the vision that they've been presented, along with those who feel a clarion call to connect and partner with the vision presented. Build what God has told you to because it's already yours, and you have the victory! The land belonged to Israel before Nehemiah declared, *"Let us arise and build."* Though the land already belonged to the children of Israel, their enemies, demonic forces, and principalities had made their presence felt. It took a conscious decision to build the "WHAT" that they were assigned to build in the "WHERE." The WHAT was what Nehemiah was assigned to build, and the WHERE was the place he knew God assigned him to build it in. There are often principalities operating in the place where God has told you to build your WHAT. However, "Understand emerging Nehemiahs: Jesus has already spoiled principalities that will attempt to combat you and your assignment" (Colossians 2:15). Let's make this declaration together: "I will put the WHAT I've been assigned to build in its WHERE!"

Nehemiah faced resistance like many people did because the enemy will try to make you feel defeated by sending opposition against WHAT God is doing through your life. So even though you are WHERE God is telling you to build, because you don't see the WHAT coming together, you give up. The enemy will fight against the WHERE, meaning geographical location, by bringing so much resistance it feels like you can't get your feet settled. At that point you start to forget about the WHAT because it seems impossible to build the WHAT in the WHERE, or you plant your WHAT in the wrong place, and it never reaches its full potential.

Psalms 40:2 (NIV) says, *"He lifted me out of the slimy pit, out of the mud and mire; he set my feet on a rock and gave me a firm place to stand."* Particularly the last part of Psalms 40:2, *"he set my feet on a rock and gave me a firm place to stand;"* God guarantees in this scripture that He sets those who are on assignment in the WHERE (which is a God place, the rock). As you stand on this firm place, the enemy, resistance, and opposition won't be able to drive you away, and discouragement will not lead you to quit. So, if one is already fulfilling their assignment of building the WHAT, then as God sets their feet on a firm place to stand, everything will fall into place. I'm telling you by the Holy Ghost that God is placing your feet on a rock to stay. Feet are a part of the body, and over our bodies is skin. God is establishing and giving you thick skin to stand in a firm place. Emerging Nehemiahs will have thick skin and will not be moved or shaken by opposition and resistance. Do not plant your WHAT in the wrong place. A wrong place is a settled position beneath God's best for one's life.

Ephesians 2:10 (NIV) says, *"For we are God's handiwork, created in Christ Jesus unto good works, which God created in Christ Jesus unto good works, which God has prepared in advanced for us to do."* As you arise and build and take on the apostolic task you've been called to, you must understand that God has created you to do great works. Notice that the latter part of Ephesians 2:10 says, *"...which God has prepared in advance for us to do."* When your time comes to arise and build, it should excite you for three reasons. One, because God has prepared you to do what He's mandating you to do. Secondly, the mandate to arise and build is God's way of declaring your time of fulfillment. Thirdly, as you are arising to build, God has also called you to shine. Isaiah 60:1 (KJV) says, *"Arise, shine; for thy light is come, and the glory of the LORD is risen upon thee."* The word light also means revelation. God will not allow you to arise and build blindly but will, through the Holy Spirit, guide you into all truth. In this era, there is coming to builders a massive and enormous amount of revelation and downloads as they fulfill the will of God for their lives. The word shine in Hebrew is "or," and it means "to be or become light." Revelation is the portion of glory carriers. An important note about glory comes from Isaiah 4:5 (KJV): *"And the Lord will create upon every dwelling place of mount Zion, and upon her assemblies, a cloud and smoke by day, and the shining of a flaming fire by night: for upon all the glory shall be a defense."* God assures protection for those arising; one, because of the finished work of Jesus Christ, and two, because of the glory of God that shields and is their protection and defense. The glory of God that is upon one's life protects them and should not be taken for granted but guarded at all costs by watching and living a life totally submitted to the Holy Spirit.

Glory causes believers to work with ease and effectiveness while protecting us from that which will attempt to stop us.

Kingdom financiers will also emerge and partner with those living out heaven's vision in the earth. In Luke 8:2-3 (NIV), the bible says *"And also some women who had been cured of evil spirits and diseases: Mary (called Magdalene) from whom seven demons had come out;, Joanna the wife of Chuza, the manager of Herod's household; Susanna; and many others. These women were helping to support them out of their own means."* These women emerged and supported the ministry of Jesus out of their own money without Him asking them to. They had seen the evidence of God and were personally changed by His ministry. Mary's name means "beloved". Joanna's name means "gift of the Lord". Susanna's name means "joy". God sent gifts and gave joy in the form of people, and there are so many other unnamed women who followed and supported His life and ministry. This is what the Lord will do for those who are obedient to Him. He will gift them with people who will support the work of God. He will also send them people who are beloved and will minister joyfully, not leaving any room for frustration in ministry. Some of the women who followed and supported Jesus were previously either demon possessed or sick and were delivered. Don't discount others because you might discount the one who God has raised up to assist you in Kingdom ministry. The next wave of Kingdom financiers will be those who truly love giving to God. I believe these women followed and supported because they wanted to be close to the anointing that was on Jesus' life. It's important to know that all we have to do is walk in the anointing that's on our life, and God will send the help that we need. The next wave of Kingdom financiers will not only be for a season, but they will be around until the end. Mary Magdalene showed up to the tomb of Jesus, and both she and Joanna testified of the resurrection of Jesus.

God spoke to Noah and told him to build an ark, and the ark sustained him during the flood. What God will tell you to construct will be what sustains you in the final days. If Nehemiahs don't build their WHAT, they will not have a sustainable place of covering when it is needed. A point to keep in mind is that what Noah built protected generations connected to him. The WHAT that you are called to construct is just that important. One reason is its significance to the Kingdom of God, and another is it will be an accomplishment that will bless generations to come. You must understand the reason God is saying to arise and build. It's because WHAT you've been mandated to build is going to save you and everything connected to you, just as it did for Noah. I'm not only referring to saving your physical life, but also saving you from frustration, depression, weariness, and insanity. This is important in a time when destruction and plagues are manifesting in the earth that are not common to man, as the rain was not common to man during Noah's day. Great collapse will occur in economies and systems that have not been structured by strategic building, but that won't affect Nehemiahs who have built their WHAT.

The Ark of God that Moses drew up the plans for and built was still around for generations to come and was beneficial and served a great purpose to those who came in contact with it. It also had different names for it. The Ark of God is eternally recorded in scripture for its significance. This is how massive the WHAT that Moses built and the WHAT that you are building is. Generations to come will benefit from it. The WHAT that you are building will also represent and produce strength, covenant, testimony, and God.

The Ark of Strength. - What you are building will be strong, so even amid adversity it will stand, and there is nothing that can affect it - Psalms 132:8.

Ark of the Covenant (Numbers 10:33). - What God is mandating you to build will be a representation of the covenant between you and God that future generations will benefit from. Every time generations to come see it, they will be reminded of God's faithfulness.

Ark Of the Testimony (Exodus 30:6) - What God is mandating you to build will be a testimony to you, for others, and it will continue to produce testimonies because of its presence and purpose in the earth.

Ark Of God (1 Samuel 3:3) - What you are building belongs to God, and whatever belongs to God that He has endorsed, He is obligated to maintain and take care of.

Nehemiah faced great resistance from many individuals, but three individuals, in particular, were the main source of his resistance: Sanballat, Tobiah, and Geshem. Emerging Nehemiahs will face similar attacks that Nehemiah himself faced; similar attacks and different ones depending on the magnitude of the WHAT and WHERE.

Sanballat means "enemy in secret, bramble, and bush". (Orr, 1915) Perhaps at one time or another, Sanballat and Nehemiah were friends, but as you arise and build, the Lord will expose the heart and motives of those who you thought were with you. You will receive resistance from those you thought would root for you. This attack will catch Nehemiahs off guard, but they must stay strong and continue to walk in their assignment. Brambles work like this because they're rough prickly shrubs and, touching them can cause pain. That is what betrayal does. Betrayal causes pain, which can halt what God wants to do through a person's life. The name Sanballat also comes from the Babylonian name Sinuballit, which means "Sin has begotten." (Bala'a, 2021) This means that Sanballat is an individual who has allowed sin to give birth. Sanballat operated in government leadership just like Nehemiah did and still opposed Nehemiah (Nehemiah 2:10). Emerging Nehemiahs will face opposition and resistance from people who are their counterparts. Sanballat, Geshem, and Tobiah were all displeased when they heard about what Nehemiah was doing. As apostolic leaders insert themselves into regions to fulfill their assignment, some people won't be able to handle their function and, as a result, will attempt to offend them.

Individuals who have the same potential as Nehemiahs will attack them as they walk in their assignment. This is what an apostolic attack looks like. It is an attack against one who's sent with miraculous power to execute their assignment. It's important to understand that it takes grace to responsibly manage what has been passed down through generations. In 1 Samuel 5, Ashdod, Gath, and Ekron were destroyed because the ark that was for Israel ended up in those places. This happened because they did not have the grace to manage what they were in possession of.

Geshem means "rainstorm". (Orr, 1915) Rain represents a natural element that occurs and falls. A rainstorm represents opposition that makes building a challenge. In building, it's important to know that not everything will go your way all the time. Rainstorms come in the form of obstacles, delays, and challenges. Yet, I believe that the Lord intentionally allows this kind of opposition, as it builds character. It teaches how to walk by faith and depend solely upon God for help and direction. Jesus assures us in John 16:33 (KJV) that life and natural occurrences will happen when He said, *"These things I have spoken unto you, that in me ye might have peace. In the world ye shall have tribulation: but be of good cheer; I have overcome the world."* Psalms 34:19 (KJV) as well says, *"Many are the afflictions of the righteous: but the LORD delivereth him out of them all."*

Tobiah means "Yahweh" or "God is good and pleasing to Jehovah". (Orr, 1915) However, when one studies Tobiah's life, they'll discover that the meaning of his name didn't match who he was. He was an influential man among the Jews and held a high position in government. Tobiah had a relationship with the High Priest Elishab. Also, Tobiah's co-conspirator Sanballat had a daughter who married Elishab's grandson, and Tobiah used this connection to his advantage and manipulated it. Tobiah's wife was the daughter of Shecaniah, who was a Judahite leader. Tobiah's son married the daughter of Meshullam, who was also a Judahite leader. So, his life was structured around people of influence, and he manipulated it to oppose Nehemiah. Tobiah represents a spirit of manipulation and control through tactical relationships to push an ungodly agenda.

Later on, in Nehemiah 4:7, not only did people who were from certain places oppose Nehemiah, but they also invited more individuals from those places to oppose Nehemiah.

Nehemiah 4:7 (KJV) – "But it came to pass, that when Sanballat, and Tobiah, and the Arabians, and the Ammonites, and the Ashdodites, heard that the walls of Jerusalem were made up, and that the breaches began to be stopped, then they were very wroth."

The Arabian people were known to be barren. Dictionary.com defines barren as not producing or incapable of producing offspring;

sterile. A barren spirit was trying to attack Nehemiah and those in Judah and Jerusalem. It was trying to get them to a place of no production. The enemy will always try to usher in barrenness against God's people to halt any kind of production.

The Ammonites were people of influence. The Ammonites were renowned people of influence who disliked the children of Israel. In a case like this, it's possible that others who they were renowned by would also dislike the children of Israel without a valid reason. An indication that you're in the will of God is when people dislike you without a cause. The Ammonites were following the guidance of one of their leaders, Tobiah, who was an Ammonite. Sanballat likewise couldn't dislike Nehemiah and the children of Israel by himself. In Nehemiah 4:2, the Bible says that Sanballat spoke before his brethren and the army of Samaria negatively about the children of Israel. A great life lesson to remember is that some people will never be satisfied with disliking a person by themselves. They will try to spew the poison they carry onto those they're connected to and have influence with. That's why one must always be careful not to associate themselves with people who will attempt to get them to think negatively about others who've done nothing to them personally. Sanballat and Tobiah were wrong about what they were spewing, but people still listened to it. Many have allowed offenses and unforgiveness to get into their hearts because of what they've heard about others, and what they've heard is a lie. Again, this is why one must be careful with who they are connected to and who and what they are influenced by.

The Ashdodites were a cohort of people known to be thieves. The bible says in John 10:10 (KJV), *"The thief cometh not, but for to steal, and to kill, and to destroy: I am come that they might have life, and that they might have it more abundantly."* This spirit of the Ashdodites works to rob you of what God has for you or what they have already obtained through a counterattack. This happened to King David in 1 Samuel 30 when the Amalekites came to Ziklag and took David's wives captive and everything in the land. It's imperative to be on guard against this spirit. The body of Christ must always be vigilant against the enemy. Nevertheless, thank God that even if the enemy robs God's people of what belongs to them, restoration will follow that.

Emerging Nehemiahs will face the spirit of manipulation from individuals who are trying to halt the work of God through their hands. This includes trying to control situations and relationships to stop progress and taint character. Emerging Nehemiahs will deal with this kind of manipulative attack by the enemy using people who are prominent in positions of power to attack them. Those in prominent positions of power can be beneficial to Nehemiahs, but instead, the enemy will use them to try and frustrate the work of God through their hands. The Lord is, however, confusing the counsel of every Ahithophel that is in an authoritative position feeding information on how to stop you. Conspiracies and manipulative attacks will not prevail against your life.

In this new era, the Lord is speaking to His people through *Isaiah 49:17 (GNT),* saying, "The builders are arising, emerging, and coming forth, and those who have been fighting against moves of God and people personally to stop them from fulfilling their destiny are being moved completely off the scene."

Isaiah 49:17 – "Those who will rebuild you are coming soon, and those who destroyed you will leave."

Despite the resistance and retaliation coming against builders, the Lord will drive away every hindrance. In biblical times God would call for the east wind to deal with enemies. There is a special word for the eastern wind, "kadim," which means "east" and deal with before. It is the direction before one if they face the sun. When this happens, the sun is in front of you. The Lord is causing the east wind to be blown and is changing the ranks and positions of those who are facing attacks. God is now putting those being attacked in front of those who are attacking.

The resistance and retaliation that Nehemiah faced while building took a strength beyond his own to overcome. It was God's power working through him.

The Apostle Paul's testimony in 2 Corinthians 11:23-28 shows that if we are going to build and do any great work for God, there will be opposition.

2 Corinthians 11:23-28 (NLT) – "²³ Are they servants of Christ? I know I sound like a madman, but I have served him far more! I have worked harder, been put in prison more often, been whipped times without number, and faced death again and again. ²⁴ Five different times the Jewish leaders gave me thirty-nine lashes. ²⁵ Three times I was beaten with rods. Once I was stoned. Three times I was shipwrecked. Once I spent a whole night and a day adrift at sea. ²⁶ I have traveled on many long journeys. I have faced danger from rivers and from robbers. I have faced danger from my own people, the Jews, as well as from the Gentiles. I have faced danger in the cities, in the deserts, and on the seas. And I have faced danger from men who claim to be believers but are not. [27] I have worked hard and long, enduring many sleepless nights. I have been hungry and thirsty and have often gone without food. I have shivered in the cold, without enough clothing to keep me warm. [28] Then, besides all this, I have the daily burden of my concern for all the churches. [29] Who is weak without my feeling that weakness? Who is led astray, and I do not burn with anger?"

The Apostle Paul had to have strong faith to endure everything that he did. In 2 Corinthians 4:7-9, the Apostle gives great insight to one as to what they should expect and know when facing these specific attacks.

2 Corinthians 4:7-9 (KJV) says,

"[7] *(But we have this treasure in earthen vessels, that the excellency of the power may be of God, and not of us).* It's important to know when facing resistance and retaliation while arising and building is that everything that we do is because of the power of God and not of our own. In the same power that we do the work of God, it is with that same power that we overcome obstacles and attacks.

⁸ (We are troubled on every side, yet not distressed; we are perplexed, but not in despair). Trouble will automatically try and attach itself to any God-assignment, but don't allow trouble to cause you to panic and get to the point where you become focused on the situation and no longer on the assignment.

⁹ (Persecuted, but not forsaken; cast down, but not destroyed). Unfair experiences and attacks will occur in many forms, but we are never alone in the battle. We may also shift for seasons and be moved to uncomfortable places, but we are never done, and it's never over. If there is breath in your body, there is time to arise and build."

As emerging Nehemiahs arise and build, their assignment will be underestimated. The bible says in Nehemiah 4:3 (KJV), *"Now Tobiah the Ammonite was by him, and he said, even that which they build, if a fox go up, he shall even break down their stone wall."* Tobiah, the master manipulator, underestimated the strength of what Nehemiah was building. Critics will think what emerging Nehemiahs are doing doesn't carry much weight until they see the manifestation of it. God allowed Nehemiah to hear what Tobiah was saying, but it didn't stop him from building. Nehemiah carried weight in the Spirit but never attempted to prove it; he continued doing what he was called to do and prayed about everything. Whenever you think you have something to prove, then it no longer becomes about God but about you and your image. Image must never be a concern for those in the Kingdom. God protects and vindicates those who don't attempt to vindicate themselves. When Joseph became second in command, you read nowhere in scripture where the Egyptians talked about Joseph as an accused rapist and ex-convict. Why? Because God protected Joseph's image in the face of people who tried to destroy him.

Relationships

The relationship that Nehemiah had with the king was a divinely orchestrated one. God is a God of intentionality, and He never does anything by coincidence. Everything that God does has a purpose. This is why we must display honor in every relationship that we have because you never know which relationship will be the conduit to cause change. This relationship that Nehemiah shared with the king is the model of what God will use to cause emerging Nehemiahs to be equipped for their assignment: favor with people in high places. However, it is very important that with these divine relationships, one doesn't become indoctrinated by a system that they've been called to. Being indoctrinated by a system you're called to is beginning to desire what that system has to offer because it seems beneficial to you.God connects you to what and who He wants you to become. Nehemiah wasn't the king's cupbearer by accident or coincidence.

God intentionally placed Nehemiah in the palace to serve as the king's cupbearer for years. For years Nehemiah watched the King up close and in a personal way. This was because God knew that one day he would lead in a governmental system. God prepared Nehemiah for the moment that he would be released into his destiny. This history-making task was to go back to Judah and Jerusalem to build and eventually become governor of Judah. If you are currently in a place right now, and it seems like your progress has been stifled, understand that God has a plan. Learn as much as you can while you are there so that when God releases you into your destiny, you will be prepared. Oftentimes people spend more time complaining and less time learning in the place where they are planted. The time that God allows one to be planted is important. God always plants so that one can grow. The danger of spending more time complaining and less time learning is that when the moment comes for one to be released to greater, they won't be ready. All because they didn't maximize the season that God was teaching them and allowing them to learn lessons in. Never despise where God currently has your life. There may be one lesson you need to learn or a relationship that you need to gain to propel your life to the next level. You may be working on a job that you consider to be mediocre, but be optimistic. You may be working for that company to learn one lesson or principle that the company does or teaches, because He's preparing you to be a business owner and to run a Fortune 500 company. Why don't you declare over your life right now that "God has purpose for my life in the place where I am right now." One word from God can change your entire life, and one relationship can shift everything for you. Nehemiah may have never imagined that one day he would be the governor of Judah, but God knew. God allowed him to be placed in a system of government and to learn what he would need to know for when he became governor. God took the foolish things of the world to confound the wise. Even in worldly systems, there are certain lessons and principles to learn from. David, before he became involved in government in Judah and Israel, was being trained on how to govern when he tended to his father's sheep. It's not always about how much you've learned as much as it is about being faithful while being trained by God. When Nehemiah got ready to take his journey to Jerusalem, he knew how governments functioned and operated. He was able to take advantage of the benefits that were available to him because he had knowledge of them. The first part of Hosea 4:6 (KJV) says, *"My people are destroyed for lack of knowledge."* God planted Nehemiah where he did to expose him to knowledge. Nehemiah could now share this information with people in the land of Judah and Jerusalem who may not have been privy to it prior to Nehemiah's emergence. Therefore, it is important to know that someone may be carrying information that you need.

Nehemiah had so much locked in him that an entire nation needed. Nehemiah was unique, and with his knowledge, he provoked an entire nation to be better holistically.

In Matthew 25:14-28, Jesus tells the parable about a man traveling into a far country, who called his servants and delivered unto them goods. The one who received two talents was just as faithful as the one who received five talents. They both were rewarded and heard the lord say, *"Well done, good and faithful servant; thou hast been faithful over a few things, I will make thee ruler over many things: enter thou into the joy of thy lord."* (Matthew 25:23 & 25) In that moment, they both were being commended for how they maximized what was given to them. The servant with the one talent was a candidate for the promise and reward, as were the servants who had received five talents and two talents, but he chose not to maximize where he was in his life with what he had. As a result, his master called him wicked and slothful, and he was stripped of even what he had been given. How many people have forfeited God's best for them because of being wicked and a complainer? This servant cost himself his next because he wasn't wise in his now, so use this example as a warning. No matter where you are or what you have, it can and will multiply as time goes on if you are faithful. His lord in Matthew

25:26 (KJV), made an interesting statement: *"His lord answered and said unto him, Thou wicked and slothful servant, thou knewest that I reap where I sowed not, and gather where I have not strawed."* The servant's excuse to his lord was that he knew how he operated, ultimately trying to shift the responsibility back on the lord. In the Kingdom of God, everything happens by the sovereignty of God and not according to how we feel. Our feelings don't give us permission to sin and will get us in trouble every time. While we may be blaming God for what didn't work out, God is looking at us saying, "You are blaming me for what I've given you all authority over and to be responsible for." God gives us what we need, and it is our job to go out and maximize it.

Walls, Gates, & Doors (Entrance & Exit Portals)

Walls:

God raised up Nehemiah not to build but to rebuild (Nehemiah 7:1) the walls of Jerusalem, which were the city's borders that protected against and stopped invasions. It is significant to understand why the walls were rebuilt and not built. God was causing His people to build upon what He already implemented. If a man builds their own wall, then they control the standard and design of the wall that they built. Walls are standards that are erected to prevent certain elements from coming in and keep components from going out. This is symbolic of God's standards being raised up for His people's protection, purpose, and purity. To restrict means to put a limit on or keep under control. God is causing walls to go up again because He wants His people's lives grounded and under control with structure.

Gates:

Nehemiah also had a mandate to rebuild the gates. Gates are places where decisions are made and where larger blessings come through. He had a mission to confront what was coming in and out of the city and the decisions being made in Jerusalem. God has begun raising a breed of watchmen who will guard the gates of regions both spiritually and physically. He has also begun to raise up a remnant who will guard their personal gates. These personal gates include the eye, ear, mind, mouth, heart, hand, and feet gates, which are discussed in detail in the chapter titled "The Forging of Something New." Personal gates receive information into them, which triggers an individual to make decisions that open doors, whether Godly or ungodly. There have been decisions made that have allowed ungodliness into people's lives. As a result, some of God's people are now in recovery mode instead of receiving mode. Thankfully, God is breaking that cycle by causing His people to confront what wants to conquer them.

Those who have the spirit of Nehemiah are those who have ascended because of affliction that God has allowed them to suffer. They will stand in the courts of heaven and hear the counsel of the Lord and make great intercession, reversing and birthing based on what they hear. They will spiritually protect families from paganism, which leads to more ungodliness. God will use gatekeepers to evict demonic entities that have had access to gates that were unsecured. Paul in 2 Corinthians 6:17 said, *"be ye separated, and touch not the unclean thing."* I believe he was saying to separate yourself from any environment that could expose you to what's not from God, and not touch any unclean thing that could open a demonic portal for the enemy to work in our lives. For example, there are gates that have been opened through demonic and ungodly activities that our forefathers participated in that we need to break. The Lord commands, and our calling demands, that we cut all evil ties. If a man touches an unclean thing, he gives it permission to operate in their life. In Judges 16:3, the Bible talks about Samson lifting the gates of the city of Gaza and taking them upon his shoulders out of the city. He completely removed the gate and doors from their position. This is an excellent example of how believers must protect themselves from being accessed. Closed, yet visible, doors are dangerous. Prophet Vince Williams once told me, "There are some doors that we have to close, but others we have to close and remove altogether, because as long as that door remains visible, there will always be a temptation to re-enter it." We see this in the story of Sampson when Delilah kept asking where his strength came from. Instead of him closing that door, he left it open, and eventually Delilah took advantage of her access. Samson delayed what should have been done long ago, and it cost him greatly. There are 12 gates that need to be built, rebuilt, or covered. Nehemiah 3.

<u>Sheep Gate</u> - The sheep gate was set aside for the sheep that were to be sacrificed. It was also essential for the spiritual well-being of the people because they conducted religious ceremonies in it. This was the first gate to be rebuilt in the book of Nehemiah. Believers are God's sheep according to Psalms 100:3, Ezekiel 34:31, Jeremiah 50:6, John 10:14, 27-28, and John 21:26. This gate signifies God rebuilding the bridge between Jesus Christ and us because of His love for people. Now that this gate has been restored, God's people can access every right and privilege as believers in Christ Jesus. The sacrifices of the sheep symbolize how we must die daily to pursue the will of God. As sheep entered in the sheep gate, they died, and as believers enter this gate, we die to our will so that we may live for Christ.

<u>Fish Gate</u> - This gate in the natural represents businesses that must be restored. God wants His people to build kingdom businesses to protect them from ungodly influences and attacks that would come against them. Spiritually, this gate is symbolic of souls that can and will be won in the last days. God is doing a great work in the area of evangelism. The Lord is causing this ministry to catch fire for the days ahead and for the harvest of souls.

Old Gate - This gate was a landmark symbolic of building upon what God already said concerning every matter. Things may be old to us, but God can still cause life to come out of it. According to Isaiah 55:11 (KJV), *"So shall my word be that goeth forth out of my mouth: it shall not return unto me void, but it shall accomplish that which I please, and it shall prosper in the thing whereto I sent it."* You can prepare yourself for what God has said about a matter by preparing and positioning yourself.

Valley Gate - This gate was utilized during the inspection of Jerusalem's walls and the land's condition.

Dung Gate - This gate was positioned to the south of Jerusalem. It was for excrement and was used to remove garbage and sewage from the city. This gate is important because, in this era, the enemy wants to convince the body of Christ through deceptive tactics to live with what will eventually destroy us. If there's no room for us, the body of Christ, to declutter ourselves of what is not like God, there will be no room for God in our lives, likewise in nations. The Lord is causing this gate to be opened because the more we use it, the more available we will become to God.

Fountain Gate - Inside this gate were reservoirs that supplied water to Jerusalem.

Water Gate - This gate was located near the fountain gate and was a vital source of water for Jerusalem. The Bible doesn't speak of this wall being rebuilt because water is a type of the Spirit. It's symbolic of God being always available to His people.

House Gate - This gate represents the movement for victory. There will be movement at the gates. This is the era of movement. God's people will experience movement and no longer live in stagnation. What hasn't moved in the past will move in this era.

East Gate - This was the first gate to open every day. The assigned gatekeeper was responsible for guarding it around the clock because of the transactions performed.

Miphkad Gate - The name "Miphkad" means "a numbering or an appointed place". (Biblehub.com) The military would gather at this gate for inspection and gathering before and after a battle. This gate was a representation of the protection of Jerusalem. It is important for this gate to be guarded because of divine strategy and intelligence for battle while it is released at the Miphkad gate. It is also symbolic of being a place of apostolic gathering to convey the future for the body of Christ. If this gate is closed, then there is no gathering or unity but a scattering. If the enemy can shut down gathering for instruction, it gives him an advantage. The gate of the gathering must be built up again, and it is vital in the days to come. In 2020, during the pandemic, this gate was closed to a degree in some places, but the Lord has caused it to be open again. Inspection will be key to ensure nothing is missed and unaccounted for in a battle or endeavor.

Ephraim Gate - Ephraim means "double fruitful". (Biblestudy.org) This gate being opened will cause God's people to be productive. The body of Christ is in an era where they will experience favor that will shift the entire trajectory of their lives. It will enable them to produce in every area of their life. God's people will build bridges to the impossible at this gate. The enemy will intentionally fight against this gate to destroy it, but the gates of hell will not prevail against what God will do at this gate.

Prison gate - This gate was used to capture those who were operating illegally. This gate was significant for legislation and implementation of what was allowed to operate within Jerusalem. This gate is important because laws and decisions can be made to release what is illegal into earth as legal to operate and function.

As walls and gates are being rebuilt in the era, the Lord is mandating that they be purified. In Nehemiah 12:30, two of the three things that the priests and Levites purified were the gates and wall. This mandate must be heeded because if gates and walls are rebuilt but not purified, then it defeats the purpose of why the gates and walls were erected in the first place. The Lord is mandating this because gates have become contaminated because of what and who has been allowed to enter them. When gates and walls are purified, it changes and evicts what's impure out and does not allow what's ungodly in. How do we as the body of Christ purify our gates and walls? In Deuteronomy 11:20, Moses told the children of Israel to write the words of the Lord upon the door post of their houses, and upon their gates. The first thing that people see before they enter a territory are the gates, walls, and doors if they are present. When there are writings on a gate, it's a reminder to who's standing at them and an announcement to who and what will attempt to gain access into them of what the standard to enter is. If the word of God is written on them, then it is a sign that the word of God is first there.

Doors:

The Hebrew word for door is "deleth," which comes from the root word dalah, meaning to draw (water). In Bible times, water was drawn from wells. To utilize a well, one would have to lower a bucket into the pit to retrieve water. Doors represent an access point where people, places, and habits enter and leave through. Similar to this concept, whenever doors are left open, it allows people to draw from or to us. Jacob told his firstborn son in Genesis 49:4 that he was "unstable as water." When doors are left open, even if the gates of our lives are secure, we invite an unstable spirit into our lives, which causes there to be instability.

In Nehemiah 3:1, Eliashib, the high priest, and his fellow priests rebuilt the sheep gate. They dedicated the wall and set up its doors. Now, why did they not only rebuild the sheep gate but also set up the doors on the wall? This was because one can secure their gates and be on guard, but if doors, entryways, and paths are left open, it can still default right decisions (gates) and information by wrong access (doors). Isaiah 61:4 (KJV) says, *"And they shall build the old wastes, they shall raise up the former desolations, and they shall repair the waste cities, the desolations of many generations."*

The word waste in Hebrew is the word "chorbah," and this word has been translated to be defined as ruined homes and cities. The Lord, in this era, is raising up an army that is called to the systems and intricate parts of old cities to build up that which is old and ruin that there may be an economic shift. The Bible in Isaiah 61:4 states, "the desolations of many generations." I believe this alludes to them rebuilding what belonged to past generations and now them.

This army will repair what belongs to them and retrieve what belonged to their forefathers. God is providing His promise of an inheritance. This is why we find the word generations; this means it includes us. When God made a covenant with Abraham, Isaac, and Jacob, it included you. There is land and territory that belongs to you that may be in a wasteful state; however, God is saying you "build". In this era, God is calling you to build up the doors that have been broken due to poor generational patterns.

He Will Prosper Us

Nehemiah 2:20 (KJV), "Then answered I them, and said unto them, The God of heaven, he will prosper us; therefore we his servants will arise and build: but ye have no portion, nor right, nor memorial, in Jerusalem."

Ephesians 1:3 (KJV) says, "Blessed be the God and Father of our Lord Jesus Christ, who hath blessed us with all spiritual blessings in heavenly places in Christ."

This means that God has already blessed His people with everything that they need. Every right and privilege as a believer in Christ Jesus has already been supplied. The word prosper in Nehemiah 2:20 is translated in Hebrew as "tsalach," and it means "to rush". (Biblehub.com) People rush because of urgency. Nehemiah told his enemies, in other words, that "The God of heaven will cause us to see rapid progress and manifestation. The Lord had already supplied Nehemiah with the resources regarding the assignment He gave him. In this dispensation and era, I believe the Lord is doing the same for us. The apostolic assignment that God has ordained for each individual or people—he will prosper them in it. We, as the body of Christ, will experience acceleration while walking in their assignment. The time that once was is no longer because we are on the eve of the return of Jesus Christ, and the prophecy of the last days is being fulfilled. Nehemiahs have been prophetically destined to emerge in an era where rapid movement is transpiring. They will see and experience rapid increases and enlargement in their lives and ministries. The problem has not been a lack of vision but provision to see the vision manifest. How did Nehemiah walk into the provision that he had? He was bold enough to ask the king for what he needed. This was a faith move on his part. When you obey God, He is obligated to provide for you. We see this in the text when the King made sure that Nehemiah lacked nothing for his assignment. Nehemiah walked in Philippians 4:19, where the Apostle Paul tells believers at the church at Philippi, who were partners with him in ministry, that his "God shall supply all your needs according to his riches in glory by Christ Jesus." When you partner with the Lord, you are eligible for this promise, not just in your assignment but for your life. The way that we partner with God is through faith and obedience. When Nehemiah was gathering the resources from different governors to build the walls of Jerusalem, he also collected resources to build himself a personal home (Nehemiah 2:8). While he was endeavoring to do God's business, the needs and wants of his personal life automatically started coming together. Jesus said in Matthew 6:33 (KJV), *"But seek ye first the kingdom of God, and his righteousness; and all these things shall be added unto you."* This is how Nehemiah lived, and the results are shown in the text. It is mandatory that emerging Nehemiahs seek first the Kingdom of God and His righteousness. A person will always become frustrated when they don't follow this Kingdom principle and seek things first rather than the Kingdom of God, whether consciously or unconsciously. As they don't see those things being added, they get discouraged and think that God isn't coming through for them. Prosperity is automatic for one in the place of their assignment. I believe also that poverty and prosperity can't coexist in the same place.

There is much to do for the Kingdom in the last days, and God is releasing a grace on His people to prosper in everything that they do. According to Psalms 1:3, *"everything that we do will prosper."* Psalms 1:3 has so many declarations for us to fulfill everything that we've been called to do. At the beginning of this verse, it says that we shall be like a tree planted by the rivers of water. God is establishing and planting you where you will be unmovable, always abounding in the work of the Lord. The psalmist uses the term, "planted by the rivers." Why is that so important? The supernatural will always manifest by rivers. Ezekiel chapter one shows us what the prophet Ezekiel saw by the rivers of Chebar. Daniel chapter ten shows us what Daniel experienced by the river of Hedekiel. Matthew chapter three shows us the supernatural experience that happened after Jesus was baptized by John the Baptist and how the Trinity are all at work at once. The heavens were opened, and the Spirit of God came descending out of heaven with the bodily shape of a dove. The Bible tells you that you are going to bring forth fruit. John 15:2 *says, "every branch that bringeth for fruit, he purgeth it, that it may bring forth more fruit."* This is important because God is telling us that if you are producing fruit, then He purges it. This word purgeth in the Greek is the "kathairó," which means "to make clean by removing undesirable elements". (Biblehub.com) This is indicative of a reality that God desires to purify all who function in the Kingdom. God is also coming behind everything that He uses to ensure that nothing is missing, broken, or lacking. It is very important during purification that the Holy Spirit is always guiding us. We cannot do it alone because in John 15:4, Jesus tells us, *"As the branch cannot bear fruit of itself, except it abide in the vine, no more can ye, except ye abide in me."* Remember, we can't go any further than God takes us. This is one of the reasons why He deserves all the glory. The next part of Psalms 1:3 says, *"his leaf will not wither,"* which means you are going to finish strong because you are connected to the vine. Lastly, Psalms 1:3 says, *"and whatsoever you doeth shall prosper."* Everything you touch will prosper because the God of heaven will prosper you.

God didn't tell Nehemiah that He would accelerate the work: Nehemiah declared, *"The God of Heaven, he will prosper us"* out of his own faith by his prophetic voice. The declaration accelerated his apostolic assignment, and as a result the wall was completed in 52 days. This was a project that was supposed to take much longer than 52 days, but Nehemiah's prophetic declaration caused acceleration. As a result, the people as well had a wind to build the wall with rapidity. Whatever assignment the Lord has given you, understand the authority you have in your voice to complete it.

Nehemiah spoke what he believed God would do, and it was done. The Apostle Paul had this conviction and said in 2 Corinthians 4:13 (KJV), *"We having the same spirit of faith, according as it is written, I believed, and therefore have I spoken; we also believe, and therefore speak."* Believers have been given authority to speak to the future. One must be careful not to oppose themselves with their confessions. 2 Timothy 2:25 teaches us we can, and some do oppose themselves. One's confession must always be parallel to their faith, and man's faith should always be in God.

7 Questions, 7 Answers

Along with the emergence of God's people, the world will begin to inquire. There will be a spotlight projected toward this remnant, and seven specific questions will be presented. These questions are highlighted within our text, and we will discuss them in detail below:

> Nehemiah 2:19 (KJV) – *"But when Sanballat the Horonite, and Tobiah the servant, the Ammonite, and Geshem the Arabian, heard it, they laughed us to scorn, and despised us, and said, What is this thing that ye do? will ye rebel against the king?"*

> Nehemiah 4:2 (KJV) – *"And he spake before his brethren and the army of Samaria, and said, What do these feeble Jews? will they fortify themselves? will they sacrifice? will they make an end in a day? will they revive the stones out of the heaps of the rubbish which are burned?"*

Question 1: What is this that ye do?

This question was asked to challenge Nehemiah due to offense because Nehemiah 2:10 (KJV) says, *"When Sanballat the Horonite, and Tobiah the servant, the Ammonite, heard of it, it grieved them exceedingly that there was come a man to seek the welfare of the children of Israel."* They were grieved at the fact that Nehemiah cared about the children of Israel's welfare. True apostolic ministry will offend some because of the weightiness of the assignment. Nehemiah arose as a solution to a problem that had been neglected. God is sending His chosen vessels into places that others in past times had the opportunity to help but declined. As this transpires, people will become greatly offended by those whom the Lord is using because of the impact that they will have.

Answer: Our response should be John 9:4 (KJV), *"I must work the works of him that sent me, while it is day: the night cometh, when no man can work."*

John 4:34 (KJV), *"Jesus saith unto them, My meat is to do the will of him that sent me, and to finish his work."*

Question 2: Will ye rebel against the king?

This question will arise because everyone will not recognize or comprehend this next move of God. In the text, many perceived rebuilding as rebellion against the king. If you embody the spirit of Nehemiah, be aware that people will try to label Kingdom business as political business. People will also think you have been influenced by the devil because of how different this new move of God will look and be.

Answer: Our response should be John 8:29 (KJV*), "And he that sent me is with me: the Father hath not left me alone; for I do always those things that please him."* I only do what pleases God.

Question 3: What do these feeble Jews?

In other words, the world will ask what do we think that we are doing? The question will challenge the validity of the assignment.

Answer: Our response should be John 6:38 (KJV), *"For I came down from heaven, not to do mine own will, but the will of him that sent me."*

Question 4: Will they fortify themselves?

Nehemiah's enemies were asking whether they will build something that would protect themselves. The world will ask the Body of Christ if what we are doing will protect us in the days to come. It can be said that people question solutions that they have neglected to try themselves.

Answer: Our response should be Romans 8:28 (KJV), *"And we know that in all things God works for the good of those who love him, who have been called according to his purpose."*

Question 5: Will they sacrifice?

Will the Lord deliver then because of their sacrifices? This is just the way God wants it. The Lord wants the light to be directed to Him, so He can show himself as El Shaddai to His people in the face of the world.

Answer: Genesis 17:1 (NLT), *"When Abram was ninety-nine years old, the LORD appeared to him and said, 'I am El-Shaddai—'God Almighty.' Serve me faithfully and live a blameless life."*

God is El-Shaddai and will provide.

Question 6: Will they make an end in a day?

The world will ask if the work will be completed. Will they survive? As if to imply that we won't make it to the end.

Answer: Our response should be Jeremiah 29:11 (KJV), *"For I know the thoughts that I think toward you, saith the Lord, thoughts of peace, and not of evil, to give you an expected end."* God is going to give me an expected end of victory.

Philippians 1:6 (KJV), *"Being confident of this very thing, that he which hath begun a good work in you will perform it until the day of Jesus Christ."* What God starts; He finishes.

Question 7: Will they revive the stones out of the heaps of the rubbish which are burned?

The world will ask whether we can take this impossible situation of nothing and calamity and produce greatness? This question implies that this situation is impossible.

Answer: Our response should be Matthew 19:26 (NLT), *"Jesus looked at them intently and said, "Humanly speaking, it is impossible. But with God everything is possible."*

Jeremiah 32:7 (KJV), *"Behold, I am the LORD, the God of all flesh: is there any thing too hard for me?"*

Philippians 4:17 (KJV), *"I can do all things through Christ who strengthens me."*

Solutions & Strategies

Nehemiah 2:17 (KJV) – *"Then said I unto them, Ye see the distress that we are in, how Jerusalem lieth waste, and the gates thereof are burned with fire: come, and let us build up the wall of Jerusalem, that we be no more a reproach."*

Nehemiah identified the issue and presented a solution at the same time. Not only did Nehemiah identify an issue and present a solution, but he was also the answer. He was just what the region of Judah needed at that time. Emerging Nehemiahs will have answers to problems. They will also be the answer to problems. Dictionary.com defines the verb of answer as, "to act or move in response to." Dear reader, "The region that you are assigned to needs you, and you are the answer."

The Issue

Then said I unto them, Ye see the distress that we are in, how Jerusalem lieth waste, and the gates thereof are burned with fire:

Nehemiah identified the exact issue that was transpiring in Jerusalem. Oftentimes, people only acknowledge the what without ever discovering the why, which is the issue at the root of a problem. God is sending His people into regions to conquer. However, it is important to know that before one can conquer something, they must first confront it. He's also sending His people into regions and systems to evict problems that have been ingratiated in society through spiritual means, which will require physical activity at times. It is also important that before you can evict something, you must first expose it. Nehemiah, during his prayer of repentance, confronted the issues that were transpiring in Jerusalem. In chapter 2, he acts and attacks the problem. This is an important paradigm, both in the Kingdom and in life in general, to confront the why before dealing with the what. Nehemiah was a prophet and operated in the prophetic, which is God's mind revealed. If you are concerned about the region that you reside in, then make this prophetic declaration that "shifting is taking place in that region." Emerging Nehemiahs should pray for the word of knowledge to be in operation in their life and ministry. A word of knowledge reveals a fragmentary part of the mind of God concerning the past or present by the Holy Spirit. When God's people operate in the gifts of the Spirit, it makes life and ministry so much easier.

The Strategy

...come, and let us build up the wall of Jerusalem, that we be no more a reproach.

Jerusalem and the Israelites had become a reproach to other nations. Unfortunately, this is still the case today, where many locations have become a place of reproach. The reputation of some places is always attached to negativity. People avoid certain areas because of the activity that transpires, and this leads to a negative reputation. When Nehemiah said, "that we be no more a reproach," he was saying, in other words, "Let us build so that people will not have a reason to see us in a negative light." Nehemiah was arising with an answer, and the answer was to stand up for the region that God assigned him to function in. Nehemiah was saying that what has been will no longer be on my watch. As emerging Nehemiahs arise, they will stand up for the region they are assigned to and release life over it with their prophetic voice. In some instances, the problem has not been a lack of solutions and strategies for a region but an increase of people speaking about death and into a situation that they want to see life in.

2 Samuel 5:9 (NIV) – "David then took up residence in the fortress and called it the City of David. He built up the area around it, from the terraces inward."

When the Lord gives you jurisdiction in and over a region, He has given an apostolic mandate to build; it means that He's charging you to enhance it economically, socially, culturally, environmentally, and spiritually. A region should look better because you are in it. When David became king of Israel, he built up the environment and shifted the economy. One of the reasons that God gives you jurisdiction in and over a region is to change its identity. Identity is the fact of being who or what a person or thing is. When David took up residence in the fortress after becoming King of Israel, he called it the City of David. He immediately, with a prophetic voice under an apostolic mandate, gave the city a new identity. David, in Hebrew, means "beloved". Therefore, it became the city where the beloved one (David) resides and the beloved city. David created a place where people were loved. After David and his men captured Jerusalem, it was then named the capital of Israel, and it is recognized as such to this present day. David left a legacy that's still intact and recognized to this present day. God has given you a prophetic voice and apostolic authority to shift the region where you reside. You have the grace, tools, and influence to make the region you are in attractive, just like David did to the City of David when he started occupying it. This grace on your life is drawing wealth and recognition to the region where you are. Nehemiah desired to change the identity of the region that he was called to, which is why he said in Nehemiah 2:17 (KJV), *"come, and let us build up the wall of Jerusalem, that we be no more a reproach."* He was saying, "let's build the wall so that the identity of Judah and Jerusalem can shift for the better." Then the bible says in 2 Samuel 5:11 (KJV), *"And Hiram king of Tyre sent messengers to David, and cedar trees, and carpenters, and masons: and they built David an house."* Carpenters and masons, which are also builders, were sent ones. They built a foundation, which was David's house. After the builders finished building, the bible says in 2 Samuel 5:12 (KJV), *"And David perceived that the Lord had established him king over Israel."* They birthed the reality of David's destiny.

Another example that displays the power of building involves one of the best communicators of our time, Bishop T.D. Jakes. Over the course of many years, millions of people have and continue to travel to Dallas for the conferences and events that he hosts. These visitors not only attended those events but also purchased plane tickets, rented cars, and booked hotels. They ate at restaurants and bought fuel and other necessities while in Dallas. Therefore, his vision brought wealth to the city of Dallas, and the economic flow of the city was enhanced. Only God can do something like that. An entire region shifted because of one man's innovation. Now, when people hear Bishop T.D. Jakes's name attached to an event, because of the evidence of what God has done through, with, and for his life, people come to it and support it. One's name being attached to an initiative doesn't take glory away from God. It actually opens the doors for that individual to give glory to their God. God told Abram in Genesis 12:2 (NIV), *"I will make your name great, and you will be a blessing."* Therefore, it is the will of God for His children's names to be recognized by others. God is raising up a generation of people who will use this influence in the seven mountains of influence. People will know when they see a particular name that their life will be better if they encounter that person or something they're a part of. The reason being is because when they encounter that person, they're really encountering God through that person. Everyone that encountered Jesus that believed that He was who He was and could do what they needed Him to do in their lives and family members' lives was better after their encounter with Him.

God is doing something incredible in this new era that will draw people to regions that perhaps people thought that they would never go to. For instance, the Brownsville Revival that started in Pensacola, Fl at Brownsville Assemblies of God church in 1995 and lasted until 2000. It was reported that over three million people came to Pensacola, FL, to experience it. That's three million people that Pensacola never would've seen had revival not broken out. The identity of Pensacola changed when the revival broke out. People were coming to the city because of what God was doing. It was recorded that people traveled from places such as Israel, Ukraine, Argentina, Melbourne Australia, Paris France, Freetown Sierra Leone, and Germany. All because of an attraction called revival that was in the city. No matter the condition of Pensacola at that time, people came because a move of God drew them. Another example would be the Azusa Street revival that started in Los Angeles, California in 1906 and lasted until 1909. Many people were drawn to Los Angeles because of healing, miracles, and the supernatural on display. That's people that Los Angeles never would've seen had revival not broken out. The Winter Bible Seminars that Rev. Kenneth E. Hagin hosted for many years drew the masses to Tulsa, Oklahoma. That's hundreds of thousands of people that Tulsa, Oklahoma never would've seen had those seminars not been there. It was an attraction.

Prior to David conquering this territory in 2 Samuel 5, it was occupied by the Jebusites. This is because Judah failed to totally drive the Jebusites out of Jerusalem in Joshua 15:63. Joshua 15:63 (KJV), *"As for the Jebusites the inhabitants of Jerusalem, the children of Judah could not drive them out; but the Jebusites dwell with the children of Judah at Jerusalem unto this day."* Building is exciting, but it is imperative to know that you will be confronted with opposition, particularly the spirit of the Jebusites. David was the King of Israel but still didn't have physical possession of the territory that God wanted him to have. 2 Samuel 5:6 (NIV) says, *"The king and his men marched to Jerusalem to attack the Jebusites, who lived there. The Jebusites said to David, "You will not get in here; even the blind and the lame can ward you off."* They thought, "David cannot get in here." Jebusites means "treading down" and "trodden underfoot." (Abarim Publications) The kind of resistance that a person or people will face when going into a region to change its identity is a spirit that tries to tread upon what you are doing or trying to do. The Bible talks about this kind of resistance. It is a high thing that tries to exalt itself against the knowledge of God. It attempts to tread down everything you do. This is the reason Jesus teaches in Luke 10:19 (KJV), *"Behold, I give unto you power to tread on serpents and scorpions, and over all the power of the enemy: and nothing shall by any means hurt you."* Believers have the power to tread upon what attempts to tread upon them and their kingdom endeavors. The Jebusites didn't want to let David in. You won't always be accepted, but keep pushing to take territory that God has ordained for you to have. When the kingdom of darkness recognizes the changing of the guard, the enemy will try to do everything he can to prohibit it. I believe that in this new era, the Lord is causing His people to possess the gates; one translation says, "the cities of their enemies" (Genesis 22:17).

I believe you are about to enter into what man said you wouldn't enter into. Every promise, every dream, every vision, every goal! When the Jebusites said in 2 Samuel 5:6 (NIV), *"Even the blind and the lame can ward you off,"* they were speaking of false idols and gods that they had set up as a defense that had eyes but couldn't see and legs but couldn't walk because they weren't alive.

The Jebusites represented a group of people at the gates who were spiritually dead. These individuals had no vision, insight, or momentum to produce. There are those at the gates and on the walls of cities who are spiritually dead. This is tantamount to those that aren't born-again believers of Jesus Christ, just like these idols who were on the wall but not alive. These individuals have physical eyes but no vision or insight as to how to strategize to advance what they are guarding. They also have legs but can't walk, meaning they can't move or progress where they are or in what they are in. There are some towns that have never experienced a mighty move of the Spirit of God, but I believe that is about to change. This includes every place that has never experienced a mighty move of the Spirit of God in it, causing a great shifting economically. There are also places that don't have any attractions in them and have never had any major events come to them. God has sent and/or planted someone there to be the attraction as God works through them to build and bring attractions to that place to cause shift. There is someone God is sending to ignite the fire. I believe there are those who are carrying a move of God within them; they can bring the presence of God within them.

There are three types of ways that attractions will be presented and erected.

The first is by being an attraction. In the mountain of religion, Jesus is and should always be the center of attention. In the six other mountains of business, family, education, government, media, and arts and entertainment, one's name can and should be an attraction that draws wealth because of what they're doing and wherever they go. When people hear certain names, they will automatically know their credibility and want to support what God is doing in their lives.

Proverbs 22:1 (KJV) says, *"A good name is rather to be chosen than great riches, and loving favour rather than silver and gold."* When one's name is good, others know what comes along with that name, even in the religious mountain. We see this often in the Old Testament when people would seek out the prophets (seers) because of their reputation, but mainly because people knew that they would encounter God through them.

The second way an attraction will be presented is by them being built. There are those whom the Lord sends and plants in a region to build and construct what's needed in all seven mountains of influence. What they will build will be an attraction to others and attract others to the region. Those attraction(s) will enhance that region economically, socially, culturally, environmentally, and spiritually. Understand that in the religion mountain, you can't build a move of God, but you can build the infrastructure for which the move of God can be housed. An example of building attractions in a region for its enhancement is creating a business that draws people to the area. For instance, when an idea is created to build a university or a college, we see people from all walks of life come to attend or enroll. That business has therefore drawn people from everywhere to that area. God's desire and plan with attractions that are built is to cause the government of that region to shift. That's why some people move to certain places, because, they are attracted to the rules, safety, and order that are there. The mountain of arts and entertainment is important when building an attraction in a region. There are currently events worldwide around the globe that happen systematically. Some are hourly, others daily, weekly, monthly, or yearly, and some even by decades and even centuries. These events attract people and generate wealth for the region where the events are held. Believers have been called to build and advance the Kingdom of God while enhancing regions that they have been planted in.

Lastly, an attraction will be presented by being brought. There are those who carry moves of God within them who have not been planted into particular regions that they go into. They, however, have been sent by God into towns, cities, counties, states, countries, and continents to release out of them and by the Holy Spirit what is attractive. Maria Woodwerth-Etter, who lived from 1844 until 1924, was an evangelist who operated in the Pentecostalism style of ministry before it was widely recognized and embraced in the United States. She is the perfect example of what bringing an attraction looks like. Maria traveled to different cities throughout the United States, hosting meetings where many were healed and delivered. According to romans1015.com, Maria's meetings got front-page attention in major newspapers. She frequently used tents that were large enough to fit 8,000 people. Even with tents that large, there were times when she had meetings that had to be held in the open air because of the crowds. During her meeting near Alexandria, Indiana, crowds swelled to 25,000 people, which Maria testified to be common whenever she conducted meetings. Manifestations of the Holy Spirit's power that manifested in cities where she held meetings, and according to romans1015.com they were incredible. That includes the power of God being felt 50 miles around from where the meetings were being held. People were struck down by the power of God in their homes, businesses, and on the highways and laid as dead men. Demons were cast out, and physical healings were verified by medical doctors who were present at the meetings. Some people, who were under the power of God, would fall into trances sometimes lasting from 1 to 8 days. A boy at one of these meetings, after coming out of a trance, rose and started exhorting. As a result of this boy, exhorting, many wept, and 500 were saved. The police in a city where Maria was hosting a meeting had no work to do. Places shut down, and the employees attended the meetings. At times "heavenly music" was heard by people. What drew thousands of people to these meetings was what Maria brought with her: the supernatural! As it is in the mountain of religion, so it will be in other mountains of influence. In this new era, we will see a generation of purpose-driven individuals who will carry and bring attractions to different regions that they have been assigned to for all seven mountains.

When Nehemiah said, *"come,"* he was gathering those who felt the clarion call to build in the region they as well felt called to. Then he said, *"that we may build,"* as he knew he needed help building. Nehemiah's strategy was to partner with like-minded individuals who desired change as well. The region that you are in or are assigned to is waiting for you. God has released a builder's anointing on His people. We are expected to turn our passion into purpose. You may be passionate about children or the elderly, or perhaps you have a heart for those who are homeless. Whatever your passion is, understand that it is going to shift someone else's life for the better.

As it relates to prophetic ministry, all solutions and strategies come from God through revelation. A word of knowledge is great, but after you have insight about what's been revealed concerning the past or present, the word of wisdom is also important. The word of wisdom is one of the nine manifestations of the Holy Spirit that reveals insight concerning the future. Out of the word of wisdom come instructions and solutions. Emerging Nehemiahs will need to pray that the word of wisdom operates in their life and ministry. This will be key to solutions and strategies in their assignment. Those that are emerging with solutions and strategies will also have the seven spirits of God upon them, according to Isaiah 11:2.

Isaiah 11:2 (KJV) – "And the spirit of the Lord shall rest upon him, the spirit of wisdom and understanding, the spirit of counsel and might, the spirit of knowledge and of the fear of the Lord."

Spirit of the Lord: This Spirit is God Himself in and on a person's life. Solutions and strategies will come to those who have the Spirit of the Lord resting in them. Sensitivity to the Holy Spirit will be imperative to receive revelation from Him like never before.

The spirit of wisdom: This spirit will give us the ability to apply knowledge to complex situations. The wisdom that we will walk in will make us valuable to nations and systems as Solomon was to leaders and nations in 1 Kings 4:34 and 1 Kings 10:24.

1 Kings 4:34 (KJV) – "From all nations people came to listen to Solomon's wisdom, sent by all the kings of the world, who had heard of his wisdom."

1 Kings 10:24 (KJV) – "And all the earth sought to Solomon, to hear his wisdom, which God had put in his heart."

Solomon is a great example. He was chosen by God and emerged as the leader of a nation, and what he released was desired by other nations. People with wisdom don't have to force an audience. Wisdom has its own force. Also, what God is downloading inside of His people will be needed in systems in the coming days. God will open doors to allow others to see how biblical principles can make you successful in every aspect of life.

The Apostle Paul, in praying for the church at Ephesus in Ephesians 1:17 (KJV) prayed, *"That the God of our Lord Jesus Christ, the Father of glory, may give unto you the spirit of wisdom and revelation in the knowledge of him."* The spirit of revelation and wisdom allows you to know the wisdom from the mind of the Father and to walk in revelation as the Spirit of God wills to reveal. This spirit of wisdom and revelation will cause believers to see beyond their natural years and ahead of the world and time. The Lord has taught me in my prophetic journey that as a prophet, we must live in the future. The calendar day may be April, but as a prophet, I must already be in September and October. Prophets give prophetic forecasts and insight into the future. Therefore, by the time we get to September and October physically, we've already been there in the spirit realm from April because there is no time or distance in the realm. Think about this: John the revelator saw 2000 years down the road into the time that we are currently living in. This is one of the reasons why prophets must live in the Spirit. We must be able to intercept the enemy's plans, among many other things. Again, when we live in the Spirit, and as the Spirit wills, we can see and travel into the future in the Spirit to stop an attack that was going to happen. Then we come back to where we are physically. Then we get to the date that we saw that attack; it has been aborted. We need the wisdom of God so that nothing catches us off guard and that we are prepared for anything with a strategy.

The spirit of understanding: The word understanding in Hebrew is the word "binah," which originates from the word "bin" meaning to discern. (Biblehub.com) Discernment is a great tool to possess and is needed more now than ever before. It will give those arising with solutions and strategies the ability to effectively apply wisdom to situations. The Apostle Paul, in praying for the church at Ephesus in Ephesians 1:18, prayed that the eyes of their understanding would be enlightened.

Ephesians 1:18 (KJV) – "The eyes of your understanding being enlightened;"

Paul was praying that their spiritual vision would be sharpened by the Spirit of God so that they could see into the spirit realm. Those who are emerging with solutions and strategies that carry the spirit of God should pray that the eyes of their understanding are enlightened. As we pray for this, we will walk in a level of supernatural understanding.

<u>The spirit of counsel</u>: Solutions and strategies will reside with those who have the spirit of counsel. We will be able to clearly articulate a vision with a plan for others to follow.

<u>The spirit of might</u>: This spirit will assist with being practical with drawing up solutions, according to Ephesians 3:20. The spirit of might will bring about determination and confidence in the one who carries it.

Also, those who carry this spirit will function in great authority as that is the purpose of this spirit.

The Apostle Paul, in praying for the church at Ephesus in Ephesians 3:16 (KJV) prayed, *"That he would grant you, according to the riches of his glory, to be strengthened with might by his Spirit in the inner man;"*

Those with the spirit of Nehemiah should pray that they are strengthened with might by the Spirit of God in their spirits. This will cause them to have an internal strength and power from the Spirit of God. This kind of might won't allow them to quit but will cause them to walk in their authority and execute in everything.

The spirit of knowledge: They will know to be aware of and familiar with what to do in situations, whether they've done it before or not, because of the knowledge that comes from the Lord.

The Apostle Paul, in praying for the church at Ephesus in Ephesians 1, declared, in other words, that the knowledge of Christ, which was accessible to them because they were in Christ. The knowledge of Christ is a huge advantage and is all-knowing. Man will never be all-knowing, but because those who are born again and Spirit-filled are in Christ, they are connected to the all-knowing God.

Ephesians 1:17 (KJV) – "That the God of our Lord Jesus Christ, the Father of glory, may give unto you the spirit of wisdom and revelation in the knowledge of him:"

Fear of the Lord: This cohort will have a reverential fear for the Lord, and because they do, they will not compromise while presenting solutions and drawing up strategies. Sometimes people feel the need to compromise to see a solution manifest because a strategy with no room for compromise takes the nine fruits of the spirit to accomplish. (Galatians 5:22)

Audience

Exodus 11:3 (KJV) – "And the Lord gave the people favour in the sight of the Egyptians. Moreover the man Moses was very great in the land of Egypt, in the sight of Pharaoh's servants, and in the sight of the people."

When Moses emerged as a leader to the children of Israel, God gave him the ultimate platform in Egypt. First, the Bible says, "Moreover the man Moses was very great in the land of Egypt." The Lord caused Moses to be very great in the land of Egypt. The word great in Hebrew is the word "gadol." Gadol comes from the word "gadal" which means to grow up or become great. (Biblehub.com) This means that the Lord caused Moses to grow up right before the eyes of the people who only knew him as Moses that was raised in Egypt, and not the great leader that he had become. The Lord told Joshua in Joshua 3:7 (KJV), *"This day will I begin to magnify you thee in the sight of all Israel, that they may know that, as I was with Moses, so will I be with thee."* What the Lord did for Joshua at the beginning of his ministry was parallel to what He did for Moses. The authority that Moses carried impacted the whole country, Egypt's economy, and agriculture. The ten plagues that fell upon Egypt affected every system and person in the land. Moses, as a prophet, became great to a worldly government, whether those in that government wanted to accept it or not. As the world has crossed over into a new era, God's prophets and prophetic voices will be recognized as great in systems. The words that they speak will come to pass and shake systems they are appointed to within the world.

Secondly, the Lord caused Moses to be very great in the sight of Pharaoh's servants. Pharaoh's servants were indoctrinated in the system of oppression that fought against Moses while he was walking in his assignment. However, whether Pharaoh's servants wanted to acknowledge Moses's greatness or not, he was still great in their sight. Pharaoh's servants in Exodus 9 had already begun to see that word, from the Lord that came from Moses's mouth was coming to pass. In Exodus 9:20 (NIV), the Bible says, *"Those officials of Pharaoh who feared the word of the LORD hurried to bring their slaves and their livestock inside."* Some of Pharaoh's servants feared the word of the Lord that was coming from Moses's mouth. The Lord gave Moses an audience with people who didn't know the Lord, yet they feared the Word of the Lord spoken through His prophet. Moses never tried to make a name for himself, which left all the room for Pharaoh's servants to fear the word of the Lord. In this new era, the Lord will give His prophets and prophetic voices foreign platforms. We will see the words that God's prophets spoke come to pass. This will cause those who are hearing the word of the Lord to be pointed to Jesus Christ and opportunities to prepare for what's coming in the earth. This will cause people, places, and systems to be saved from destruction and failure in the days to come. God will receive the glory and be prioritized. The world is coming into a time where what people once laughed about, they will now listen to. For so long, when some people that have heard others say that things are coming in the earth, they paid it no attention. However, now people will run to Kingdom people out of a desire to know what is to come.

Exodus 7:10 (KJV) – "And Moses and Aaron went in unto Pharaoh, and they did so as the Lord had commanded: and Aaron cast down his rod before Pharaoh, and before his servants, and it became a serpent."

Moses and Aaron had a platform before a king. I believe that God is going to cause His prophets, who are called to nations and governments, to stand before heads of nations to speak the mind of God. As they were standing on the platform that God had given them, their audience increased because of what they were able to demonstrate. Aaron cast down his rod before Pharaoh and his servants, and it became a serpent. At that moment Pharaoh's servants witnessed the power of God. That moment opened their hearts, and eventually they feared the word of the Lord. In this next season, everybody may not listen, but the Lord will cause people to be influenced by what the body of Christ demonstrates.

Lastly, the Lord made Moses great in the sight of all of the Egyptians. Moses became great in the sight of people who were used to experiencing the magicians of Egypt revealing what they wouldn't have known except by a divine outlet and performing wonders through the practice of sorcery. Whether the Egyptians wanted to acknowledge Moses's greatness or not, he was still great in their sight. The authority that Moses walked in affected the Egyptians' bodies and families. As Moses operated under the power of God while speaking, Aaron was the one doing. In this new era, the Lord causes those who are emerging as prophetic voices to be great in the sight of all people. As the world shifts and shakes, God will use this time for His prophets and prophet voices who are great to arise and shine. *1 John 4:4 (KJV) says, "Ye are of God, little children, and have overcome them: because greater is he that is in you, than he that is in the world."* John wrote this to believers during a time when he was making them aware of the false prophets and false spirits that could and would deceive. I believe that Christ, the greater one that lives in the believer, is what will cause the believer to overcome the false, by showing forth true power because when the truth speaks, the false must become silent. What was false was on display until the truth came forth through Moses to shut it down. Moses operated in this power stated in 1 John as God used him to demonstrate His judgment on Egypt. It affected the state, condition, and living of those who lived in Egypt, not just Pharaoh's servants. A present example of this would be COVID-19. The entire world has been affected by this virus. The flow of people's everyday life was interrupted and forced people to pause, which the Lord used, I believe, as an opportunity to cause His prophets to be heard. The 2020 pandemic that swept the entire globe showed that when a people's flow is interrupted, it causes their eyes to be opened and perspectives to change.

A Prevailing Spirit

Nehemiah 6:18 (KJV) – "For there were many in Judah sworn unto him, because he was the son in law of Shechaniah the son of Arah; and his son Johanan had taken the daughter of Meshullam the son of Berechiah."

Nehemiah had to contend with an evil prevailing spirit in the land while endeavoring to fulfill his assignment from the Lord. A prevailing spirit is an entity that houses itself in a person. It tries to control a person, place, or thing in a region through the influence. An example can be seen in Matthew 8:28 (KJV), *"And when he was come to the other side into the country of the Gergesenes, there met him two possessed with devils, coming out of the tombs, exceeding fierce, so that no man might pass by that way."* This legion, or prevailing spirit, tried to control the area by the tombs so that none might pass that way and through that region. Tobiah tried to do this to Nehemiah when he entered Judah and Jerusalem through fierce intimidation. He despised that Nehemiah came into the region to build. As a result, he attempted to hinder Nehemiah's function through people he still had influence over and an audience within Judah. The difference between this spirit and a principality is that a principality doesn't need a body to function, while spirits do.

Many in Judah were still committed and sworn to Tobiah, and he was the very one fighting against the progress of the land that was coming through the work that God was doing through Nehemiah. They were sworn to someone who was fighting against the person who embodied the solution they needed. Only an oxymoron joins themselves to anything or anyone that's trying to destroy what they need. Did these individuals in the land of Judah who were sworn unto Tobiah really want to see change come to their region, or did their loyalty to Tobiah cause them to dislike Nehemiah and miss what God wanted to do through him, which was going to shift their life? Nehemiah knew that there were many in the land of Judah still sworn to Tobiah. He felt the resistance of this prevailing spirit. I'm sure the individuals in the land of Judah who were still sworn to Tobiah saw the great need for deliverance into the land. Connected to this prevailing spirit is the spirit of pride. Pride sees chaos and continues to function without conviction. The effects and aftershocks of Tobiah's presence, decisions, and influence in Judah were felt long after he was in the land. This also means that Nehemiah wasn't as respected and regarded for who he was and what he meant to the land of Judah. This happens in the life of a prophet. Jesus said, "*I came onto my own, and they received me not.*" The Apostle Paul gave insight as to why and how this spirit is able to operate in a person when speaking to the church in Corinth in 2 Corinthians 4:4 (KJV) when he said, *"In whom the god of this world hath blinded the minds of them which believe not, lest the light of the glorious gospel of Christ, who is the image of God, should shine upon them."*

To not believe is to spiritually oppose what God has declared. Whenever this happens, it gives the enemy a license to cause people to be blind to what God is doing. The eyes of the people who were sworn to Tobiah were blind to what God was doing through Nehemiah's life. They didn't believe in what God was doing through Nehemiah. If they would've believed in and seen Nehemiah for who he was, they wouldn't have been trying, whether consciously or unconsciously, to frustrate whom God sent to help their future. The danger of unbelief is that without faith, it's impossible to please God. The tragedy, however, of unbelief is that it causes you to miss God and what He's doing through a person, in a place, or in a particular system. All because you couldn't and didn't accept it. The enemy wanted to keep division in the land of Judah through this prevailing spirit. He didn't want the people in the land of Judah to get a revelation of who Nehemiah was, and he didn't want them to participate. This is the reason the enemy fights against people hearing the gospel, because it penetrates the heart and transforms lives. If these individuals who were sworn to Tobiah had true revelation, they would have had eyes to see the truth. Nehemiah had to know that his assignment was from God to build in a region. He knew that those within the region were loyal to someone who was fighting against what God was doing through his life. Yet, in fighting against Nehemiah, they were fighting against what would've helped them. Just look at how crafty the enemy is; he'll let you dislike who God has sent to be a voice of deliverance. Nehemiah, being completely aware of this resistance, had to walk in love and stay in faith and focused. He had the capacity to build while knowing information that could've discouraged him to stop, yet his passion would not allow him. The next prophet that would have stepped into this region and country of Gergesenes in Matthew 8 would have had to deal with this prevailing spirit because it never left the land. This displays the power of a prevailing spirit. Nehemiah had to deal with this again during his second return to Jerusalem. Tobiah returned to the land after Nehemiah left and used his influence to have the high priest, Elishab, prepare a room for him and his items in the courts of the house of God. The Apostle Paul confronted the church of Corinthians in 2 Corinthians 12:11 because there were super-apostles among the church of Corinth, and their influence on the church of Corinth bothered the

Apostle Paul because it caused them to undermine what he was saying. A prevailing spirit contends with truth and those of truth in a region or place.

Emerging Nehemiahs are assigned to a specific group of people, but only some of those people will feel called to their voice. They must stay focused without allowing offense to get into their hearts. If one isn't careful, a few critics can discourage them to abandon the entire assignment. When they do this, they are also abandoning the ones who do or would've received them. It's important to emphasize that not everyone in Judah was sworn to Tobiah. There were individuals in Judah that felt called to Nehemiah's voice; otherwise, he wouldn't have been able to galvanize support to build the wall. A lesson that God will teach individuals in life and ministry is how to perfect their love walk. One of the ways God will do this is for them to be planted in an environment where people reject and dishonor them. However, in that same environment where they're being dishonored, there are individuals who honor, serve, and support what God is doing in their lives. In this God will teach you two lessons in one. To love those that dishonor you and keep moving forward with those who are with and honor you because if the enemy can cause you to exhaust all your energy with who's not with you, you'll get stuck there and forget about who's with you and not move forward. The assignment of this evil prevailing spirit is to alter one's focus, so their attention is on what's irrelevant and away from what is vital to their progress. Nehemiah 6:19 (KJV), *"Also they reported his good deeds before me, and uttered my words to him. And Tobiah sent letters to put me in fear."*

Two issues were transpiring within Judah:

First, the people of Judah were reporting Tobiah's good deeds to Nehemiah. The people of Judah were reporting irrelevant information to Nehemiah, possibly to discourage him in his assignment because the bible says they were Tobiah's good deeds. Nehemiah could've easily questioned God as the Prophet Jeremiah did in Jeremiah 12:1 (NIV), *"Why does the way of the wicked prosper? Why do all the faithless live at ease?"* This was also inevitably an attempt to cause Nehemiah to focus on what was not important and that which didn't pertain to his purpose. The more time that the enemy can keep you focused on what doesn't matter, the more time he'll keep your attention away from what is important. One must settle in their mind that they are not a garbage disposal; therefore, they can't consume garbage. They also can't afford to allow anything close to them and in their ears that doesn't pertain to their purpose because they've got too much riding on what they're endeavoring to do for Jesus. The Bible tells us in Matthew 10:16 (KJV), *"Behold, I send you forth as sheep in the midst of wolves: be ye therefore wise as serpents, and harmless as doves."* A great quality about doves is their eyesight. When I'm as harmless as a dove, I can see what you're plotting on me a mile away and still love you. In addition to this, understand that love is not a license to give ear to who and what will disrupt your destiny. *"Wise as serpents,"* meaning I'm using wisdom by following the word of God along with the guidance of the Holy Spirit and godly counsel to keep myself from what will disrupt my peace and progress. To be as *"harmless as doves,"* means I love everyone and do good to everyone. I would like to reiterate again that the root is the spirit of distraction, and its purpose was to alter Nehemiah's focus to derail him from destiny. If the enemy can distract you, then he can cause you to derail from your course. Once a train is derailed, it can't move forward. Also, everyone that is onboard a derailed train immediately becomes in danger of not being able to function properly because of the derailment. Therefore, if the enemy can cause derailment for one, then he can disrupt them and stop their function. This, however, also stops those connected and assigned to the life and voice of the one who is derailed. Everything on board a train symbolizes everything that's on a person's life not being able to function, manifest, and operate because of their lack of focus and/or derailment. The gifts, anointing, grace, and mantle that God has put on the inside and on them can't benefit others when the one carrying it has a lack of focus and is living selfishly.

If Nehemiah's focus had been altered, it would have affected the whole nation. It was much bigger than him. One's determination and decision to stay focused can save an entire nation. One's focus can cause a person to experience and encounter God in a moment that they may really need Him in. Being sensitive to the Holy Spirit as to what to say, or not say, or do, or not do in those moments also makes all the difference in sealing a person's deliverance with any hindrances. Also, one's decision not to stay focused can cost someone their life, literally. It can also rob someone of a moment that God wanted to give them by and through using that individual who wasn't focused. So, people who decide to live selfishly and unfocused are thieves who rob people of moments with God. However, thank God that God always has someone somewhere who will listen and obey Him. It is true that one person's breakthrough and deliverance is tied to another's obedience.

The second issue I want to address is that the people of Judah were reporting Nehemiah's words to Tobiah. God allowed Nehemiah to know and hear that they were talking about him. Them reporting Nehemiah's words to Tobiah was a form of gossip. To gossip is to unnecessarily take information, whether true or false, from one source to another with impure and alternative motives. An evil prevailing spirit will always attempt to prevail against apostolic and prophetic leaders through people operating under the spirit of gossip. Years ago, Apostle Dannie Williams tells the story about him hearing critics in the community saying erroneous things about him that he really didn't want to hear. One day, God spoke to him and said, "I'm allowing you to hear this while you're small so that when I ask you to do something big for me, you'll do it with no problem." Nehemiah only replied to his enemies once in scripture, in Nehemiah 6:6-7. This means he had enough wisdom to know that he couldn't control what the heathens were saying about him. However, he could control the energy he exerted towards this situation. This reminds me of King David in Psalms 7:8 (NKJV), who prayed to God and asked Him to *"vindicate him according to his righteousness and the integrity that is in me."* Believers don't have to prove their integrity. God will always vindicate those who don't try to vindicate themselves.

Another assignment of this prevailing spirit is to cause believers to fall prey to the spirit of rejection. Every person at some point in their life will be confronted with the spirit of rejection in some form. Remember, Nehemiah was confronted with rejection but prevailed. If one isn't careful and responds incorrectly to this attack from this prevailing spirit, in the end, the spirit of rejection will have a hold of them. Nehemiah didn't allow rejection to grip his heart, which would've caused him to deviate from God's will and standards. He kept doing what he believed God called him to do, and he had success. God desires for us to have success, resilience, and longevity. It's always a tragedy when one starts off successfully, but then an event transpires that hinders them from longevity. It is an even greater tragedy to be successful at what God called you to do, have longevity in it, but towards the end of it something transpires that causes you to only be remembered as a shell of what you once were. In Isaiah 14:16-18 (KJV), the Bible says, *"They that see thee shall narrowly look upon thee, and consider thee, saying, Is this the man that made the earth to tremble, that did shake kingdoms. That made the world as a wilderness, and destroyed the cities thereof; that opened not the house of his prisoners? All the kings of the nations, even all of them, lie in glory, every one in his own house."* Isaiah's prophecy in Isaiah 14:16-18 alludes to the reality of those who once saw Lucifer as being successful at doing what he was created for. However, he is remembered now as the one who fell from where he was. As great as Lucifer was before his fall, it didn't matter once he fell. All of it was only a memory when he was looked at after the fall.

Saul was confronted with rejection, and he allowed it to grip his heart. When Saul saw the men scattering from him in 1 Samuel 13:11, he compromised and didn't follow the instructions of the Prophet Samuel (1 Samuel 15:28). Nehemiah faced something similar but didn't compromise. Emerging Nehemiahs must be content in knowing that not everyone will be for them and that some people are seasonal and won't be with them for their entire journey. Therefore, when we see men scattering, we must remain settled. If the enemy can get believers to allow rejection to grip their hearts, it will be easier for them to compromise.

5 Fold Gift

Ephesians 4:11 (KJV) – "And he gave some, apostles; and some, prophets; and some, evangelists; and some, pastors and teachers;"

The hand of the Lord was upon Nehemiah according to Nehemiah 2:20. In addition to the hand of the Lord being upon Nehemiah, the hand of the Lord was functioning in the earth through Nehemiah as he was a type of fivefold ministry gift.

Apostle

Nehemiah 2:5 (KJV) – "And I said unto the king, If it please the king, and if thy servant have found favour in thy sight, that thou wouldest send me unto Judah, unto the city of my fathers' sepulchres, that I may build it."

The Greek word for apostle is apostolos, meaning a sent one with miraculous power. (Biblehub.com) Apostles are sent to a specific people or place to fulfill a purpose. Nehemiah was a sent one. He was on assignment to build up a city and people. He created a hub of protection and provision whereby the people can experience the presence and power of God.

Nehemiah 2:5 (KJV), *"…send me unto Judah, unto the city of my fathers' sepulchres, that I may build it."*

He was sent with authority and blessings from the king, which caused opportunities to be open for him. When the Lord sends you, He connects you with people. Their conduits provide provision and protection just as the king did for Nehemiah. The king sending Nehemiah is a type of God, the King sending forth his apostles. People in earth simply affirm what God has already done. Nehemiah was sent with a word through letters that the king gave him to give to the different governors that he would encounter along his journey. When apostles are sent, they carry the word of the one who sent them. Nehemiah began his apostolic assignment with a team that could handle the magnitude of his assignment. Nehemiah 2:9, *"Now the king had sent captains of the army and horsemen with me."* Nehemiah had a group that consisted of militaristic leaders. They were skilled and knew how to engage in battle and war. This is what God will surround emerging Nehemiahs with: people who know how to engage in spiritual warfare. Horsemen were also of great assistance to Nehemiah because they moved hindrances out of the way. They were drivers, armor bearers, servers, and assistants to help bring ease and peace. It will be critical for those carrying the spirit of Nehemiah to have watchmen within their inner circle.

In this next era, it will be important to utilize wisdom and apostolic intelligence. For example, Nehemiah didn't just start building in Judah or Jerusalem. He did spiritual mapping of the land to better understand the assignment he was getting ready to take. It is imperative to never go on an assignment blindly but to do research to understand the history of your assigned region. One must be prepared for principalities that exist in an area, as noted in the Prevailing Spirit chapter. Tobiah, Geshem, and Sanballat represented principalities that function in a region, and when the principalities are dealt with, the work will be done with ease.

Prophet

Nehemiah 8:9-10 (KJV) – "And Nehemiah, which is the Tirshatha, and Ezra the priest the scribe, and the Levites that taught the people, said unto all the people, This day is holy unto the Lord your God; mourn not, nor weep. For all the people wept, when they heard the words of the law. Then he said unto them, Go your way, eat the fat, and drink the sweet, and send portions unto them for whom nothing is prepared: for this day is holy unto our Lord: neither be ye sorry; for the joy of the Lord is your strength."

Prophets not only hear the word of the Lord, but they see as well, as seers. I believe that Nehemiah saw the walls of Jerusalem built before it was physically erected with just a blueprint. Now, while scripture doesn't classify Nehemiah as a seer, seeing the blueprint for the walls and work done before it was done is one of a seer's functions. Seers see a thing from the end, then build from the beginning to birth what they saw from the end. There is an emergence of seers; prophets who can see a thing in the spirit before it manifests in time. Prophets look into desolate places, see what God is calling forth out of eternity, and then build it in time. This is because prophets are not only called to prophesy but also to build what they see. There is a remnant of prophets emerging with a clear vision, faith, and zeal to build what they've seen in eternity. Nehemiah was what I called the Visionary Prophet and the Building Prophet.

The Visionary Prophet sees something in the natural like he saw it in the spirit realm, though it hasn't yet become tangible. Nehemiah's vision was so clear that he had a sense of urgency regarding the work! This is the kind of focus we will see from the emerging Nehemiahs. They will work without delay or procrastination as the grace of God gives them a wind. An example of a Building Prophet is Noah. He was prophetic in his utterance and serious in action. A Building Prophet effectively utilizes all resources made available to them to build what they've seen or heard in the realm of the spirit without delay. Noah began to build immediately after he heard God say it was going to rain. Nehemiah as well began to build immediately once he knew that he was sent to build. Nehemiah, like Noah, utilized resources made available from God through people. I believe we will operate under the same anointing; we will build with a sense of urgency and accuracy.

Teacher

There will be a new level of grace poured out to teach the Bible with supernatural revelation. These instructors will share valuable insight regarding government, business, finance, and much more. These teachers will also have a great sphere of influence, enabling them to teach to the masses. Nehemiah taught those assigned to his voice how to live victoriously through biblical principles. We will begin to see emerging teachers disguised in Babylonian systems. For instance, more mentors, life coaches, and counselors will arise to represent the Kingdom of God and witness about Jesus Christ. Along with those disguised, we will see many unapologetically present themselves as teachers of God in systems they are called to. According to Nehemiah 8, many teachers emerged and taught God's people. God used Moses to deliver Israel from Egypt and

Pharaoh's bondage. David was King Saul's deliverer when evil spirits came over him. These teachers will have the grace to teach people things that will cause cycles of bondage and oppression to be broken off their lives. This includes what has them bound spiritually, mentally, emotionally, financially, and educationally that affect the house of God and them in Babylonian systems.

Pastor

Nehemiah 4:9 (KJV) – "Nevertheless we made our prayer unto our God, and set a watch against them day and night, because of them."

Nehemiah 4:18-20 (KJV) – "For the builders, every one had his sword girded by his side, and so builded. And he that sounded the trumpet was by me. And I said unto the nobles, and to the rulers, and to the rest of the people, The work is great and large, and we are separated upon the wall, one far from another. In what place therefore ye hear the sound of the trumpet, resort ye thither unto us: our God shall fight for us."

John 10:1 (KJV) – "Verily, verily, I say unto you, He that entereth not by the door into the sheepfold, but climbeth up some other way, the same is a thief and a robber."

These pastors that are emerging will have a spirit of discernment to see who's attempting to gain illegal access to God's people to destroy them.

John 10:3 (KJV) – "To him the porter openeth; and the sheep hear his voice: and he calleth his own sheep by name, and leadeth them out."

These pastors that are emerging will be accepted and received. Those assigned to them will embrace their voice and respect it as a messenger from God.

Evangelist

Nehemiah 5:16 (KJV) – "Yea, also I continued in the work of this wall, neither bought we any land: and all my servants were gathered thither unto the work."

From the time Nehemiah left the palace at Shushan to reaching Judah and eventually leaving, he spent time gathering people for the purposes of God through witness that what he was doing was of God. This is what evangelists do, they proclaim the gospel of Christ to win the lost and therefore gather them to be turned over to a pastor for building up. Nehemiah 10:28 (NIV), *"The rest of the people—priests, Levites, gatekeepers, musicians, temple servants and all who separated themselves from the neighboring peoples for the sake of the Law of God, together with their wives and all their sons and daughters who are able to understand."* The word evangelist means "a bringer of good news or glad tidings". (Biblehub.com) During Nehemiah's dispensation, the gospel of Jesus Christ had not yet arrived, but Nehemiah did bring good news about God. Nehemiah modeled in the Old Testament a shadow of the New Testament. He gathered and led the third wave of exiles back to Jerusalem. In Nehemiah 10:28, even though Nehemiah had returned to Persia, we see the masses accept what God was doing in their lives and separate themselves from ungodliness. This is what happens when a believer accepts Jesus Christ as their personal Lord and Savior: they divorce cultural abominations. Nehemiah 10:1 (BSB) says, *"Now these were the ones who sealed the document…"* The document that was being sealed was from the children of Israel's commitment to God to live for Him. In Nehemiah 9:38 (KJV) it says, *"And because of all this we make a sure covenant, and write it; and our princes,*

Levites, and priests, seal unto it." There was a sealing that took place, which is symbolic of a New Testament type of the Holy Spirit. Once a person believes in Jesus Christ and accepts Him as Lord and Savior, their spirits are born again, and the Spirit of God seals them. Ephesians 4:30 (KJV) says, *"And grieve not the holy Spirit of God, whereby ye are sealed unto the day of redemption."* Emerging Nehemiahs will preach the good news of Jesus Christ and point people to Jesus in everything they do. 2 Corinthians 6:17 (KJV) teaches the church of Corinthians to, *"Wherefore come out from among them, and be ye separate, and touch not the unclean thing: and I will receive you."* This is what happens when a person becomes born again; they consecrate and separate themselves. They no longer touch or engage in things that are not God's best for them. This will be the result of the manifestation of souls that will come to Jesus Christ in this era.

After Nehemiah and the people finished building the walls, in Nehemiah 7:4, Nehemiah then saw that the city was spacious and large, but there weren't many people in it. The houses within the city weren't built. God then put it in Nehemiah's heart to assemble the nobles and officials to find out exactly who came back from Jerusalem when Zerubbabel led the first captives of Babylon. In this, Nehemiah could find a way to repopulate Jerusalem. A great portion of the Jews were dwelling in cities and towns in the country but not in Jerusalem. Nehemiah had the assignment to prepare a place for them for what they were about to step into. God is one assembling and calling His people back to their rightful place. Why wasn't Nehemiah's first assignment to gather the Jews out of their different towns and cities and then build? God is intentional in why He led Nehemiah to build first and then gather. God wasn't interested in His people leaving one place of hardship in Babylon and stepping into another place of disorder in Jerusalem. People have sometimes looked at the church and asked themselves this question, due to what they experienced and witnessed. "Why would I leave the world, get saved, and come to church and experience what I did in the world?" This call that Nehemiah made was a type of evangelism. Therefore, the Lord is calling for order and structure to come back to the church.

The Table

Nehemiah 5:17 (KJV) – "Moreover there were at my an hundred and fifty of the Jews and rulers, beside those that came unto us from among the heathen that are about us."

A table is a place where one welcomes an audience of people or a person. It also represents a position and place of authority. Nehemiah had a table that God trusted him with. Nehemiah ruled over an entire nation, but he allowed 150 people to sit at his table. One had to be trustworthy to see Nehemiah behind closed doors. Only trustworthy people can be integral enough to keep what they hear in intimate settings confidential.

The primary assignment of those who get close to leaders is to cover them. Prophet Vince Williams once used the example of how Ham, the son of Noah, saw his father's nakedness and went out and told his brothers. He was close to his father, who was his leader as well, but he couldn't be trusted because he exposed what he was supposed to cover. This caused his seed to be cursed. Shem and Japheth, Noah's younger sons, according to Genesis 9:23 (KJV), *"took a garment, and laid it upon both their shoulders, and went backward, and covered the nakedness of their father; and their faces were backward, and they saw not their father's nakedness."* They covered what could've been exposed and because they did, Shem was blessed, and Japheth was enlarged by God.

In life, when the Lord trusts man with a table, they must be careful who they allow to have a seat at that table. Everybody cannot and should not have that kind of access to a man's life. In my own personal journey with the Lord, I've learned that everybody shouldn't have access to my life. I shouldn't allow everybody to walk in and out of my life because of the revelation that is being released from my table. There is some revelation that God allows man to release in public, and some that God only permits a man to release in private from his table. There was a lot of revelation that Jesus released to the public, but some He only released and expounded upon to His 12 apostles. Samuel, the prophet, controlled who sat at his table. The bible says in 1 Samuel 9:19 that Samuel invited Saul up into the high place to eat with him. Saul never would've had access to Samuel's table had Samuel never invited him. You control your environment by limiting what is around you. Apostolic and prophetic voices must use discernment and inquire of the Lord as to who can have access to their table, even as it relates to family.

One must never take for granted if God allows them to have a seat at a Nehemiah or any leader's table. Nehemiah was a powerful man that God blessed and favored, and everyone who sat at his table had access to everything at his table. Therefore, all who had access to his table had been promoted to a greater place. This can be spiritual or physical elevation and promotion or spiritual and physical promotion and elevation. Nehemiah wasn't just a leader; he was a door for them; a door for them to reach greater places and obtain greater blessings.

Ephesians 6:12

Ephesians 6:12 (KJV) – "For we wrestle not against flesh and blood, but against principalities, against powers, against the rulers of the darkness of this world, against spiritual wickedness in high places."

But Against Principalities

The word principality is translated in the Greek as "arché," which means "beginning or origin". (Biblehub.com) Arché originates from the Greek word "archó" which means "to rule or to begin". When an apostolic or prophetic is building in territories, regions, and within the jurisdiction that they have, they must know that they are contending with what has been since the beginning. Therefore, they must go back to the origin of whatever they are dealing with to successfully get victory over what is ruling where they have been sent. When the angel came and talked with Daniel in Daniel 10, he revealed to him exactly what was withstanding him, which was the prince of Persia. Even though Michael, one of the chief angels, was released to fight against the prince of Persia in this particular instance. The prophetic paradigm of this story is that Daniel, as a prophet, knew exactly what was withstanding him. He knew exactly what was ruling in the territory that he was in, and because he knew what was withstanding him, if he had to fight against it then he could do so successfully.

God wants His children to have revelation to understand what they are contending against, but more importantly, the origin of what they are contending against. Merriam-webster defines origin as the point at which something begins or rises, or from which it derives. Never just see what's manifesting on the surface, always go back to the root of where it started to understand what exactly is manifesting, why it's manifesting and conquer it. In Nehemiah 2:20 (KJV), "said but ye have no portion, nor right, nor memorial, in Jerusalem." Sanballat, Tobiah, and Geshem are types of principalities whose function shows how principalities operate. When Nehemiah told Sanballat, Tobiah, and Geshem that "you have no portion, right, or memorial to Jerusalem," he was confronting the origin of what was happening, which was the why. He knew who and what he was contending against; therefore, he was able to go back to the origin of what was attempting to function where he was called to. Notice, Nehemiah told them that they had no right to Jerusalem. When someone has a right to something, according to dictionary.com, they have a just or legal claim on something or on some action. Nehemiah was disrupting ungodly function against a region by telling them that they couldn't legally operate and have any part of what was happening in Jerusalem.

Against Powers

The word powers in the original text is the word authorities, and in Greek is "exousia," which means "power to act or authority". (Biblehub.com) Exousia is also used as weight, regarding moral authority, influence, and jurisdiction. This word is associated in scripture with those who were in physical positions of power. The enemy has a certain amount of power, yet he doesn't have power over the believers in the body of Christ. He's been delegated some authority to operate on the earth as the god of this world and in the spirit realm. That's why Jesus in Luke 10:19 (KJV) says, *"Behold, I give unto you power to tread upon serpents and scorpions, and over all the power of the enemy: and nothing shall by any means hurt you."* Jesus acknowledges that the enemy has power. Believers wouldn't need power to fight someone powerless. The spiritual powers of the enemy manifested physically to work against Nehemiah's life and the work that God had called him to do. However, it was unable to defeat Nehemiah because of the hand of the Lord upon his life.

Against the Rulers of the Darkness of this World

Darkness of this world is translated "kosmokratór" in Greek and means "a ruler of this world". (Biblehub.com) Kosmos in Greek means order and world, and this was used in association with kingdoms and constitutions. Krateó means "to be strong, and to rule".

In John 14:30, Satan - the prince of this world, is translated in Greek as "archon," meaning ruler or chief. It's used in describing a lead person. In scripture, this was a member of the Jewish elders who held positions of power within the Jewish government.

Jesus, when giving the great commission to His apostles in Mark 16 (KJV), told them to, *"Go into all the world."* The word world here in Mark 16 is translated in Greek as the word "kosmos." Yes, God wants man to go throughout the earth preaching the gospel and evangelizing, but He has also sent His children into particular kosmos. Therefore, God has called and commissioned His people to the very system that will fight against them. Nehemiah was sent into the kosmos. God implemented him into governmental systems throughout his life.

Against Spiritual Wickedness in High Places

The word spiritual is "pneumatikos" in the Greek. (Biblehub.com) It's made up of two words. "Pneuma" means "wind, breath, spirit", and relates to spiritual things. Tikos is added to verbal stems to form adjectives. High places is also translated as heavenly places. The Apostle Paul in 2 Corinthians 13:2-4 spoke about having an out-of-body experience in which he was caught up into the third heaven. There he heard unspeakable words that weren't lawful for him to utter. If the Apostle Paul speaks of a third heaven, then there is a first and second heaven. The Bible in multiple places speaks of heavens, plural. Genesis 1:1 (NIV) says, *"In the beginning God created the heavens"* (plural) and the earth. Hebrews 4:14 says, *"Seeing then that we have a great high priest, that is passed into the heavens* (plural)*, Jesus the Son of God, let us hold fast our profession."*

The first heaven is the immediate atmosphere above man that can be seen with the natural eye that contains the sun, moon, and stars. Matthew 6:26 (KJV) says*, "Behold the fowls of the air: for they sow not, neither do they reap, nor gather into barns; yet your heavenly Father feedeth them. Are ye not much better than they?"* The word air in Matthew 6:26 is the Greek word "ouranos," and it means "heaven". (Biblehub.com) In Genesis 1:20 the bible speaks about the fowls flying above the earth in the firmament of the heaven. Earth is translated as the ground, and heaven is the Hebrew word "shamayim," which means "sky". This information shows that birds don't fly out of the earth into heaven where God is. The first heaven that the bible is suggesting is right above man that can be seen.

The second heaven is the place where Satan's throne is. This is where principalities, demons, and fallen angels operate. Ephesians 6:12 speaks about, *"spiritual wickedness in the heavenly places."* Ephesians 2:2 (NIV) says, *"in which you used to live when you followed the ways of this world and of the ruler of the kingdom of the air, the spirit who is now at work in those who are disobedient."* Satan is the ruler of the kingdom of the air. When the Bible speaks about the air, it's speaking of what's above. Therefore, Satan has a kingdom, and it is above. Also, the Apostle Paul in Ephesians 1:19-23 (KJV), while praying for the church at Ephesus, explained in his prayer the power that both God and the body of Christ have over everything that they wrestle against in Ephesians 6:12.

The third heaven, according to the Apostle Paul is the throne of God and the celestial heaven where God dwells.

[19] And what is the exceeding greatness of his power to us-ward who believe, according to the working of his mighty power, [20] Which he wrought in Christ, when he raised him from the dead, and set him at his own right hand in the heavenly places, [21] Far above all principality, and power, and might, and dominion, and every

name that is named, not only in this world, but also in that which is to come [22] *And hath put all things under his feet, and gave him to be the head over all things to the church* [23] *Which is his body, the fulness of him that filleth all in all.*

A Builder's Praise

Nehemiah 4:10 (KJV) – "And Judah said, the strength of the bearers of burdens is decayed, and there is much rubbish; so that we are not able to build the wall."

In Nehemiah 4:10, Judah began to confess defeat because of the resistance that God's people were facing while building the wall. The circumstances that they saw are significant of the reality that every believer, at some point in their life, will be faced with circumstances that will challenge their faith. Judah confessing defeat is significant of the reality that the enemy is always looking for a door to come through and steal a builder's praise. Judah means "praise". The enemy was after the builder's praise because he knows that if he causes people to lose their praise, he can disarm them. Praise is a weapon that causes people to overcome. In 2nd Chronicles chapter 20, it was Judah's praise that caused them to be delivered out of the hands of the children of Ammon, Moab, and mount Seir who had come up against them. Faith overcomes (1 John 5:4). The reason people praise is because of their faith in God. There are a couple of things that praise does that I want to point out. First, praise energizes individuals in moments of uncertainty and causes them to focus on God more than on the circumstances at hand.

Secondly, praise confuses the enemy. Most times if a person or people loses their praise, complaining and pity aren't too far behind. Judah confessed defeat immediately after the children of Israel had just corporately prayed in Nehemiah 4:9.

Prayer is meaningless without faith and belief in God. Judah went through the rituals of prayer, but deep down they believed that they were defeated. Judah in Nehemiah 4:10 showed actions that alluded to their compromise. First, their feelings. Their feelings spoke louder than praise. When Judah declared that "the strength of the bearers of burdens is decayed," they were confessing defeat. Feelings can be so dangerous because they can govern man's decisions. Unfortunately, people have made decisions based on how they felt in a moment or in a temporary place where they are now living with the permanent consequences. The Apostle Paul in 1 Corinthians 9:27 (KJV) said, *"But I keep under my body, and bring it into subjection: lest that by any means, when I have preached to others, I myself should be a castaway."* Man is a spirit that possesses a soul and lives in a body, according to 1 Thessalonians 5:17. Therefore, all three times that the Apostle Paul said "I" in 1 Corinthians 9:27, he was speaking of his spirit, which was the real him, bringing his body, which is his flesh, into subjection. He said this because he refused to do a great work in serving God's people to then become a castaway and miss God Himself. As believers, we must always allow our spirits to govern our flesh. There will be times when we will have to tell our feelings to take a backseat. The enemy would love nothing more than for God's builders to focus on their feelings and miss God.

Second, when Judah acknowledged that *"there is much rubbish,"* they were confessing their circumstances. Judah was allowing the circumstances that were presenting itself to affect their ability to build. Circumstances will always present itself, however, when circumstances present itself, we as the body of Christ, must present our faith. The Apostle Paul in 2 Corinthians 5:7 (KJV) said, *"For we walk by faith, not by sight."* Paul knew and understood that what man sees can affect how they feel, and feelings can dominate a man's decision and override his faith. Feelings and circumstances told them what they couldn't do, so that we are not able to build the wall. Nehemiah had a great mandate from God, but Judah allowed their feelings, because of circumstances, to pull them into disbelief. Builders and those who are walking in their assignments must know that they can't allow how they feel in a moment to cause them to lose momentum. Momentum can be easy to lose and hard to build back up. Builders and believers must know they have the victory in Christ Jesus. 1 Corinthians 15:57 says, *"But thanks be to God, which giveth us the victory through our Lord Jesus Christ."* David in Psalms 34:1 (KJV) said, *"I will bless the Lord at times, his praise shall continually be in my mouth."* David wrote Psalms 34 during a time when he was on the run from King Saul, who was trying to take his life. This caused him to have to leave his home country and dwell among the Philistines. Even in a difficult place when David's circumstances were horrendous, he vowed to bless the Lord at all times and release praise out of his mouth. Naturally, when a man goes through situations that are difficult, the feeling to praise God isn't always there, but David vowed to praise to God because it gives voice to victory.

David in Psalms 42:5 (KJV) was troubled in his soul and asked, *"Why art thou cast down, O my soul? and why are thou disquieted in me?"* Immediately after David said this, he followed it in the verse by saying, *"hope thou in God for shall I yet praise for the help of his countenance."* This attitude carried David through many hard places. That's why he said in Psalms 27:13 (NKJV), *"I would have lost heart, unless I had believed That I would see the goodness of the LORD In the land of the living."* The praise that caused David to keep going is the praise that builders need while on assignment for the Lord to keep going despite the turbulence that will present itself. Praise is so powerful that it can shift one's environment and atmosphere.

Lastly, Judah said, *"so that we are not able to build the wall,"* which was them declaring that they can't finish the wall. This was one of the worst confessions that they could've made and one of the worst confessions that a believer can make. The Apostle Paul in Philippians 4:17(KJV) said, *"I can do all things through Christ which strengtheneth me."* When a believer says that they can't do something, it's because their feelings and circumstances have caused them to believe they have to do what they're doing in their own strength. What Judah should've said was, "we can't in our strength alone *(the strength of the bearers of burdens is decayed),* but with God's help we can." Doubt always has a clear pathway when people attempt to make the impossible happen in their own strength. We need God no matter what. Don't limit the supernatural by saying what you can't do in defeat, because it deletes God from the total equation. God is a God of the impossible because, according to Matthew 19:26 (NIV), Jesus said, *"With man this is impossible, but with God all things are possible."* You keep God a part of every equation by living by Matthew 19:26 and understanding that you can't, but He can, therefore, you can through His power.

In Nehemiah 4:10, Judah is speaking of their defeat, and in Nehemiah 4:11, their adversaries discuss planning an attack on them. Why are these verses in that order? Judah opened a door for the enemy by talking about defeat. Fear and unbelief open demonic portals. Fear is a pause button that paralyzes people, and God can do absolutely nothing in that environment. The bible says in Matthew 13:58 (KJV), *"Now He did not many works there because of their unbelief."* Jesus Himself couldn't work in an environment of unbelief.

Don't Fear

Nehemiah 6:13-14 (KJV) – "Therefore was he hired, that I should be afraid, and do so, and sin, and that they might have matter for an evil report, that they might reproach me. 14 My God, think thou upon Tobiah and Sanballat according to these their works, and on the prophetess Noadiah, and the rest of the prophets, that would have put me in fear."

Nehemiah 6:19 (KJV) – "Also they reported his good deeds before me, and uttered my words to him. And Tobiah sent letters to put me in fear."

There is an emergence of believers who will not allow people and their opinions to intimidate them from walking in their assignment. How many times have we, as people, allowed what others think about us to affect what we endeavored to do in life in any capacity? Fear stops you from pursuing your dreams and aspirations. The bible gives man a direct command not to fear in Isaiah 41:10 (KJV), *"Fear thou not; for I am with thee: be not dismayed; for I am thy God: I will strengthen thee; yea, I will help thee; yea, I will uphold thee with the right hand of my righteousness."* The Apostle Paul, in writing to the church of Rome in Romans 8:15 (KJV), said *"For ye have not received the spirit of bondage again to fear; but ye have received the Spirit of adoption, whereby we cry, Abba, Father."* Fear is a sin, and the penalty is bondage. According to Revelation 21:8, the fearful will have their part in the lake of fire and brimstone. Therefore, it's imperative that man guards himself from fear. Nehemiah's enemies used tactics of fear to try to get him to abandon his assignment. If one is not careful, they will find themselves questioning the will of God because of fear. For instance, they'll ask questions like, "What if I endeavor to do what God is telling me to do and it doesn't work out?" or "What if I'm obedient to God and people don't listen to me?" Remember, Nehemiah was called to systems, and taking on that task took faith. He could've easily said, "I've never led in this capacity, and no one will listen to me." Nehemiah had the ability to walk by faith where God was sending him, and nothing was able to stop him at any point in his life. I believe this is the word for you who are reading this. God has been preparing you for what you have been called to do, and nothing will stop you. You're more qualified than you think. Be cautious because the enemy will try to make you fearful of what others think about you and your assignment. Another example is *Job 3:25 (KJV), "For the thing which I greatly feared is come upon me, and that which I was afraid of is come unto me."* If we open the door to fear, the enemy knows that whatever we fear will eventually manifest because fear attracts. A tactic of the enemy is to keep us focusing solely on our fears while we miss what our fears attract. The whole assignment of the people that tried to stop Nehemiah was to get him to do three things, according to Nehemiah 6:3:

Nehemiah 6:3 (KJV) "And I sent messengers unto them, saying, I am doing a great work, so that I cannot come down: why should the work cease, whilst I leave it, and come down to you?"

1. Get him to stop fulfilling his assignment, (*why should the work cease*),

The enemy's greatest desire and mission is to get an individual to stop fulfilling their assignment in the earth. This is because the enemy understands that if a man walks in their God-assignment, it does damage to the kingdom of darkness. So, one of the strategies of the enemy to get people to stop fulfilling their God assignment is through fear and intimidation. This fear and intimidation come through the enemy himself speaking to you, waging warfare against you, and through people that he uses.

2. Leave the place or post or his assignment (*whilst I leave it*)

The enemy also has deceived many people by causing them to leave or abandon the place of their assignment, and once they do it they get frustrated and think that God is no longer with them. It's not that God has abandoned them; it's that they've left that place of assignment. Whatever post or place you've been assigned to, don't leave it.

3. Step into a place that God has not called you to (*come down to you.*)

The enemy will always try to get a person into a place they aren't called to because it takes you outside of your grace and the grace assigned to cover you. Ono was the place that Tobiah and Sanballat tried to get Nehemiah to step into. Ono in Hebrew originates from the word "on," and it means "wealth". (Biblehub.com) If a person steps into Ono, it's because money has become their focus, and their motives are impure. Once they're in a place where they aren't supposed to be, iniquity will begin to drive their decisions. Then they feel hopeless because they feel like they may never recover from their decision and make it back to repentance. That's how imperative it is not to step into Ono.

God is currently exposing strategies like this so that His people do not fall for or into any trap of the enemy. Never give ear to voices that God has not assigned to your life, and don't be moved by the words of your critics. Sanballat sending letters to Nehemiah was him using the mountain of media to promote fear. This is the mountain that the enemy will use in the last days to put people in fear. Nehemiah did eventually read the letter that Sanballat sent through his servant to come to Ono, not that he was wrong to read it. However, it opened a door for Sanballat and others to try to intimidate Nehemiah because now his ear was open to what people had to say. I have learned, especially in this world of technology and social media, not to read and give credence to what people may write. Apostle Dannie Williams has said for many years, "He who has your ear has your destiny." The one who you give your ear to the most will dominate your belief system. Make sure God has declared your season is up in a place and not your fleshly desires.

What are you currently not doing in the earth relative to your Kingdom assignment that you are supposed to be doing? Have you allowed the opinions of people to intimidate you into backing down from what you were born to do? It's important to know that people will always have their opinions, but don't allow that to stop you from fulfilling the call of God upon your life. Don't allow the Sanballat and Tobiah assigned to your life from hell to cause you to quit. Your assignment is too great.

Let's dig deeper into Nehemiah 6:2-8. Nehemiah faced a lot of challenges while walking in his assignment. One of the objectives of this resistance was to topple Nehemiah from a place where God had elevated him to. If the enemy can't stop you with resistance, he then has a strategy to try to topple you to crumble through retaliation. Though Nehemiah was facing the challenges that were because of his assignment, the spirit of excellence that rested on him agitated them. No matter who it is or what it is, believers must live by the kind of attitude that King David had in Psalms 27:3 (KJV), *"Though an army besiege me, my heart will not fear; though war break out against me, even then I will be confident."* Emerging Nehemiahs must have the mindset through assurance that when God has elevated them to a place, there's no opposition that can trump it. They must also always operate in the spirit of excellence to protect the integrity of the Lord's work. Apostolic leaders will have to deal with assassinations against their character and ministries. Nehemiah was lied on and called self-righteous and a rebel. God is raising up a generation of believers that will emerge and be labeled by some as self-righteous and rebellious. Self-righteous because they know who they are in Christ Jesus and aren't intimidated by people who are attempting to intimidate them, which intimidates people. A rebel because what they are doing is so big, outside of the box, new and different that people won't be able to wrap their minds around it being God. Nehemiah had already told the people in Nehemiah 4:14 (KJV), *"Be not ye afraid of them."* Not only did he preach this to the people, he himself walked and couldn't be moved by resistance.

Nehemiah 6:16 (KJV) – "And it came to pass, that when all our enemies heard thereof, and all the heathen that were about us saw these things, they were much cast down in their own eyes: for they perceived that this work was wrought of our God."

This move of God will gain momentum in three ways:

First, people will hear about this move of God through word of mouth. Years ago, I had an assignment at a church. I was getting ready to post it on social media, and the Lord spoke to me and said, "My glory will endorse itself." The world will hear about what God is doing in these last days. People will hear about wonderful acts of the Lord and His moving. I believe moves happening on one side of the globe will be heard on the other side of the globe with or without social media.

The world will hear about the greatness of God as He demonstrates His goodness. This will create conversation among people who haven't accepted Jesus Christ as their personal Lord and Savior in arenas where the name of Jesus Christ hasn't been welcomed. This will create a curiosity to see if what they've heard about is true. God's people will see God manifested in their lives as He uses us as instruments for His plans and purposes in the earth.

Secondly, Nehemiah's enemies saw what God had done for His servant and what He had built. People will see and witness this move of the Spirit and great work with their own eyes. In 2 Kings 7:1-2, Elisha gave a prophecy concerning Samaria and then said, *"Behold, thou shalt see it thine own eyes."* Miracles, signs, and wonders will be witnessed and seen by many. John 6:2 will be the motto and will draw attention in this current era. John 6:2 (AMP) says, *"A large crowd was following Him because they had seen the signs (attesting miracles) which He continually performed on those who were sick."* People followed Jesus Christ because of evidence. One of the attractions that will draw people to Jesus Christ in this era will be glory. The evidence of fulfillment and manifestations will cause many to run after God. The world will not be able to deny that Jesus Christ is Lord. God allowed the attention to be on Nehemiah so that when the work was done, they would know that God was with Nehemiah. God is not intimidated by the attention being on His church. Jesus, in Matthew 11:4 (NLT), told John the Baptist's disciples, *"Go back to John and tell him what you have heard and seen."* This was Jesus's response to John the Baptist sending his disciples to put pressure on Jesus because he was in prison. Jesus didn't try to defend who He was when John the Baptist tried to put pressure on Him to do something. He didn't try to perform under pressure to prove Himself. It is imperative that every believer masters the skill of resisting the urge to perform under pressure. Especially in moments when it seems like that's the only thing that will silence those who are applying pressure. Performance is for entertainment. Whenever people think God isn't enough, they attempt to entertain people by forcing what is not from God in the name of God. Jesus, in Matthew 11:4, simply pointed to what the Father, God, was doing by alluding to what was happening in that era that He was in. Darkness is the prerequisite to all eyes being on God and His church. God will show forth His power, and people will see it. The world will see great healing, deliverances, creative miracles, signs, and wonders.

Lastly, this move of God will be so new and powerful that people will perceive this is a move of God. People will hear and see things and perceive that could have only happened through divine intervention from God. This will be our opportunity to evangelize to the lost about Jesus Christ. When the Apostle Paul came into Athens in Acts 17, he was on apostolic assignment. While there, he went into the marketplace system, and he met with people in the market daily. The Apostle Paul also disputed with the Jews daily in the synagogue concerning the gospel of Jesus Christ. In Acts 17:18 you see certain philosophers of the Epicureans and the Stoicks begin to question the gospel that the Apostle Paul was preaching. However, in Acts 17:19 (KJV), you see these same people, out of curiosity about what the Apostle Paul was saying, brought him to Areopagus saying, *"May we know what is the new doctrine, whereof thou speakest, is."* This is because they began to perceive within themselves that even though what they are hearing is different, it just may be true and from God. In Acts 17:20, these people began to express to the Apostle Paul their desire to know the meaning behind what he was preaching. After the Apostle Paul preached his great message at Athens, some believed, and others wanted to hear what he said again. People will perceive and discern the sovereign hand of our God. In Nehemiah 6:16, the very enemies who were opposing Nehemiah after the wall was completed perceived that work was "wrought of God."

When the Lord asks us to do a work for Him, sometimes we will say, "Nobody knows who I am." Not understanding that if we do what He's asking us to, He will send the people who are assigned to us. In this, those who the enemy has sent against your assignment to try to stop what God called you to do will HEAR, SEE, and PERCEIVE that God is with you.

This new era and dispensation will be known as the hear, see, and perceive era and dispensation. It will be known as such because this is an era of fulfillment. As God performs miracles for and through His people, sinners will witness it. Only God is powerful enough to use the same thing to speak to His people and their enemies at the same time.

Nehemiah 6:11 (NLT) – "But I replied, "Should someone in my position run from danger? Should someone in my position enter the Temple to save his life? No, I won't do it!""

Emerging Nehemiahs will be bold and will not run when persecution arises against them. They are built for tough times, equipped with strength, and never caving into pressure because the Bible says in Proverbs 24:10 (KJV), *"If thou faint in the day of adversity, thy strength is small."* Nehemiah asked Shemaiah two questions in Nehemiah 6:11 (NLT), *"Should someone in my position run from danger?"* and *"Should someone in my position enter the Temple to save his life?"* Nehemiah's answer to Shemaiah's question was, "No, I won't do it!"

Nehemiah refused to run away and hide from trouble. He understood the position that he was in because he said, "should someone in his position." Nehemiah knew that God had elevated him and that he couldn't run from this adversity. I believe this is because he knew this came along with the assignment. It's imperative to know that when God elevates you to a certain position, you can't avoid the warfare that comes with that position. You simply have to be confident in knowing who you are in Christ Jesus. You must know that you have victory before the battle manifests because the bible says in 2 Corinthians 2:14 (KJV), *"Now thanks be unto God, which always causeth us to triumph in Christ."* Nehemiah also perceived in Nehemiah 6:12 that God had not sent Shemaiah to help him. Nehemiah was sensitive enough to know that this battle wasn't something he should engage in in any capacity or give his energy to. Some battles don't deserve your energy or time. The faster one learns this, the less time they will spend running to and defending themselves, and the more time they will spend fulfilling their Kingdom assignment. Nehemiah, knowing this, didn't go to the temple as Shemaiah had suggested, and his life was saved. An unnecessary battle fought that's avoidable can be the thing that kills you. The Prophetess Nadiah and the rest of the prophets were probably all influenced by Tobiah and

Sanballat to intimidate Nehemiah. Nehemiah walked in faith, while Shemiah, Nadiah, and the rest of the prophets promoted fear. If a prophet is promoting fear, God is not leading them. God's prophets practice and promote faith, while false prophets promote fear.

Just like in the days of Nehemiah, Jesus said that false prophets would arise in the last days. Matthew 24:13 (KJV), *"And many false prophets shall rise, and shall deceive many."* Emerging Nehemiahs will have to deal with false prophets while walking in their assignments. However, there is a confrontation in this era of Kingdom people confronting darkness. A great confrontation that will transpire will be between Nehemiahs, who are true prophets and prophetic voices, and false prophets, whose assignment is to usher people into deception. Understand that false prophets aren't those who release a prophecy, and it doesn't come to pass. They may have been a presumptuous prophet (Deuteronomy 18:22). Dr. Shaun Ferguson once said that "False prophets challenge true prophets' authority." Noadiah and the rest of the prophets tried to put Nehemiah in fear. False prophets attempt to put people in fear through manipulation to stop them from fulfilling their assignment. It is deception to prevent the true prophets from fulfilling the call of God upon their lives. The assignment of a false prophet is to get one's eyes off God through fear and to also direct attention onto themselves. If anything someone says brings fear, it is not God. The Apostle Paul, in speaking to the church at Rome in Romans 10:8, called the bible *"The word of faith."* Therefore, no matter what is revealed from the mouth of a prophet, faith should come and never fear. 2 Timothy 1:7 (KJV) says, *"For God hath not given us the spirit of fear; but of power, and of love, and of a sound mind."*

Usually, these kinds of people become intimidated because others' lives and ministries are seemingly prospering while their lives and ministries appear to be at a standstill. People being intimidated by others has caused much division in the body of Christ. The scripture doesn't even record the names of these other prophets that Nehemiah referred to in his prayer. Only Shemaiah and Noadiah. This means that they didn't necessarily have the recognition that Nehemiah had. A great question that one should ask themselves is, "Can you handle nobody knowing your name and not be intimidated; therefore, you don't attempt to intimidate others?" Don't ever think small of your assignment and envy the ones who seemingly have a great assignment with more recognition. Nehemiah's assignment was great, and he was fully functioning in his assignment. His progress was undeniable; what he completed in 52 days was absolutely considered impossible. Imagine how people who thought small of themselves and their assignment handled seeing Nehemiah show up on the scene and galvanizing men to complete the wall in 52 days. All of it while combating the forces of darkness.

These prophets were not there when Nehemiah was serving the king; they simply saw the results of everything that he had walked through leading up to that point and were intimidated by it. They probably failed to acknowledge Nehemiah's work ethic and qualities. The bible teaches in Proverbs 29:25 (NLT), *"Fearing people is a dangerous trap, but trusting the LORD means safety."* To put great value in other people's opinions about you limits you from moving forward. Fearing people and their opinions will literally cause one to self-destruct their life. How Jesus lived His life is a perfect example of how one can avoid fearing people and their opinions. In the latter part of John 8:39 (KJV), Jesus said, *"….for I do always those things that please him."* Jesus lived His life to please His Father as He walked in His assignment to fulfill purpose. This concept kept Jesus from being in bondage to the opinions of the Pharisees, Sadducees, Scribes, and others who challenged Him. Always live to please God and Him alone.

Nehemiah, also perceiving that Shemaiah had been hired by Sanballat and Tobiah in Nehemiah 6:12, exposes why the prophetic must be purified in this era. There was a culture of people in Nehemiah's time who were manipulating the prophetic without regret.

The Selfless Leader (Governmental Gatekeepers)

A selfless leader is someone who has a heart for people and is always concerned about others before themselves.

A governmental gatekeeper is a Kingdom person that God plants on the governmental mountain where decisions are being made. This gatekeeper, with their influence, vocalizes God's mind to create change or bring correction.

There is a false narrative that has been gravitated towards by many for so long, and it must be confronted. The false narrative that I'm alluding says that God's people shouldn't be involved in politics and shouldn't be politicians. This is a lie! Nehemiah was a politician, assigned by God to be a politician, and prior to that, God allowed him to serve a king in government for where He was taking him. One should just be mindful that if they are called to that arena, their political voice should never speak louder than their prophetic voice. They must know that they've been planted in that system by God to uphold the standards of God within their sphere of influence. Governmental gatekeepers are emerging and are being planted in governmental systems. The main attribute of governmental gatekeepers is their selflessness. People, especially believers, can't pray for change and then, when God raises up governmental gatekeepers who are of the Kingdom of God, shun them. When people do that, they are opposing who and what has been sent to be delivered. There is such a great demand for believers in government. Sure, God can move upon the heart of an unrighteous person to do what He desires to be done in the earth. The Bible says in Proverbs 21:1 (KJV), *"The king's heart is in the hand of the Lord, as the rivers of water: he turneth it whithersoever he will."* Why, however, pray for change knowing that there are unrighteous people who will oppose what God desires to do in governmental positions, and be content with them in those positions? However, shun Kingdom governmental gatekeepers whose hearts are influenced by the Word of God and Spirit of God to make decisions that will be beneficial to mankind as a whole. There are laws that are currently intact in countries that keep people in bondage and prevent them from embracing their freedom in God. The answer to many prayers about change may just be Nehemiah and governmental gatekeepers who are of the Kingdom of God. God doesn't want any earthly system to function without a believer in authority.

I've had the privilege and opportunity to watch a governmental gatekeeper up close and in a personal way. My Pastor, Dr. Shaun

Ferguson is both a pastor and a councilman in the city of Rockledge, Florida. The two of us had a conversation on record about how important governmental gatekeepers are.

This was our conversation:

Me: Dr. Shaun, you currently serve as both the pastor of a local church and a city councilman in the city of Rockledge. What is it like being a leader in both mountains (religion and government mountain) at once?

Dr. Shaun: I find it to be an extreme honor that God would allow me to serve in these two capacities. The Word of God says in Proverbs 29:2 (NKJV), "When the righteous are in authority, the people rejoice; But when a wicked man rules, the people groan." I believe more than in any other time, we need righteous people that will take on a responsibility, walking in the power of God and totally submitted to the Holy Spirit to be in places of authority. This way, there are godly people present who don't have a spirit of greed or selfish ambitions and who are doing what's best for the citizens of this nation, in states, and locally as laws are being made. So again, it's an honor and a joy for me to serve in the capacity that I do in government.

Me: I've heard you talk about the criticism that you were faced with specifically from those within the faith community when you decided to run for city councilman. Why do you think you were criticized by those within the faith community when you decided to run for city councilman?

Dr. Shaun: I think the criticism came because of a lack of understanding. Many people don't see whereas believers we should be involved in politics. Well, I've never seen myself as a politician! I see myself as a public servant. That means I'm there to serve the public at the discretion of Holy Spirit. I was ridiculed by believers because they felt as though because I'm a pastor, therefore that I should not be involved in any type of local, state, or national politics. I find that to be completely untrue because again, the bible tells that the righteous must take on the responsibility of being in a place of authority. Why? So that people will rejoice and be in a position to live out their best life because there are godly people in a place of authority. Not just praying, but legislating laws that will be in agreement with the Word of God and God's plans for His people.

Me: How have you been able to operate in government and not become indoctrinated with the system that you are called to?

Dr. Shaun: I think it's really simple. It's because as a believer I have a relationship with the Holy Spirit. The most important thing that I can walk in through my personal relationship with the Lord is to live out His plan and purpose not only for my life, but to be in a place to live it out on behalf of generations to come and those who are present in today's world. I've been able to keep myself in a place of purity and holiness simply once again because of my relationship with the Lord. That is the most important thing. It's more important than me being famous and gaining popularity with people. It is to make sure that my relationship with the Lord stays intact. If I follow God, then I'll truly live out not only what God has in store for me but also for the lives of others who are connected to me.

Me: Dr. Shaun, I've seen you in Tallahassee, Florida in the state's capitol building praying, reading scripture, releasing the Word of the Lord corporately, laying hands, and even prophesying personally into the lives of your contemporaries in government. What were those experiences like and how important are those moments in the mountain of government?

Dr. Shaun: Wow! They were absolutely amazing experiences. However, we have to remember that these government officials and legislators that I've had the opportunity to minister to, they are people just like we are. They are husbands, wives, fathers, and mothers. They hurt, they have disappointments, and they're rejected, so they have a lot on their shoulders. Some of them run businesses, and others have secular jobs, so they carry a lot of weight. So, I was pleasantly surprised and excited that everyone that we stopped and had the opportunity to minister to was completely open to it. Not one legislator rejected us. Not one person said, "I don't want or need prayer." They were all open to the moving of the Spirit of God and word of prophecy. Again, people in today's world are hurting, and they just need some people to be bold enough to move forward and do what God has called them to do.

Me: Being in Tallahassee as much as you are, at the forefront as decisions are made concerning the state of Florida, how much MORE appreciative are you that God has placed you, a godly man, there?

Dr. Shaun: I'm truly appreciative, but I'm humbled more than anything else. I'm truly reminded why I'm there. It's because I have a mandate from God to be there. God has placed me! God has spoken to me! God has given very clear directions that this is where He wants me to be. To know that and to do what I'm doing is truly humbling because I don't go in the name of Shaun Ferguson. I don't go because I'm some smart intellectual. I rest in the power of God upon my life to accomplish what He's called me to. There's a scripture that I hold on to, Acts 17:28 (KJV), where it says, "For in him we live, and move, and have our being." So, there's no way that I can say it's anything that I'm doing; it's only because of what God is doing through me. Therefore, I'm truly humbled to serve.

Me: You are the voice of God to many and a prophetic voice in the faith community. How do you balance having both a prophetic and political voice while never allowing your political voice to speak louder than your prophetic voice?

Dr. Shaun: I am a son and man of God, first. That's primary. That's the most important thing in my life. So, no matter where I go, God goes with me. No matter what platform I may be on in that moment, I always go in the name of the Lord Jesus Christ, understanding that I represent him. That is always foremost and the most important thing in my life, that I go in His name. I'm also always reminded that I'm there to serve people. I'm a public servant and it's important that I always recognize that I'm not going for any personal agenda that I have. I'm going to represent the Kingdom of God, the people of God, the citizens of our local community, state, and other platforms that God will grant me. As a public servant, I'm there only to serve the people and in place to be a voice for the people and those who don't have a voice for themselves.

(End of Conversation)

The main attribute of Nehemiah was his selflessness. In this hour and era, there will be a great emergence of leaders who are selfless. God will cause them to have great influence in their area of function. These areas include but are not limited to prime ministers, ministers, governors of states, state representatives, mayors, and councilmen. This will consist of those who have the influence to cause change and implement laws, rules, and systems that will cause a change in regions, cities, areas, and neighborhoods that have been forsaken and underserved. Jesus prayed, *"Thy Kingdom come, thy will be done on earth as it is in heaven."* This is because it is God's will that earth becomes what heaven already is. In the Kingdom of God, the poor are not forsaken, and selfishness is not accepted. We will see a true invasion of the Kingdom of God in the earth in the days to come as God uses His chosen in politics. Emerging Nehemiahs carry the Kingdom of God within them (Luke 17:21). Matthew 9:36 (NLT), *"When he saw the crowds, he had compassion on them because they were confused and helpless, like sheep without a shepherd."*

When Jesus saw the crowd, He was moved to provide for them. If one is only or more interested in receiving from the audience that follows them than they are in giving to them, they operate in selfishness. The Bible teaches us that it is more blessed to give than to receive. That does not only involve money but also time, talents, and treasure. The only way Jesus could see the crowd was He had to be focused on His assignment. Matthew 20:28 (NIV) says, *"just as the Son of Man did not come to be served, but to serve, and to give his life as a ransom for many."* Jesus could've easily been focused on the fact that He had to go to the cross and suffer many things. He could've focused on the fact that one of His disciples was stealing the money and would betray Him. Despite all that He was faced with, He still decided to focus His eyes on those who needed Him. Those who needed Jesus were confused. The word confused is defined in Merriam-webster as disoriented with regard to one's sense of time, place, or identity. Helpless is defined in Merriam-webster as lacking protection or support. Jesus served a people that lacked support and protection because of His selflessness. The people were like sheep without a shepherd. A true leader is moved and concerned by those who have no leadership. Understand this: God takes leadership very seriously in life in the Kingdom of God. That's why in Jeremiah 3:15 (KJV), he told Israel that *"And I will give you pastors according to mine heart."* The Bible says the people were like sheep, and this moved Jesus because sheep don't have a leader but will follow whatever sheep moves first. In 2006 in eastern Turkey, 400 sheep lost their lives because one sheep tried to cross a 15 feet ravine, and the rest followed that one sheep. This is the reason why selfless leadership is important because people may only be one decision away from shipwrecking. Nehemiah had such a reverential fear for God that it drove his decisions. The Bible teaches us in Proverbs 9:10 (KJV), *"The fear of the LORD is the beginning of wisdom: and the knowledge of the holy is understanding."* Wisdom is the ability to apply knowledge. When Nehemiah embarked in his role as governor, he nor anyone in his cabinet ate the bread of the governor. Nehemiah refused to live at the expense of others' inconvenience. This possibly included an allowance that Nehemiah refused to accept. Nehemiah, like the Apostle Paul, became all things to all men to reach those whom he was serving. (1 Corinthians 9:22, KJV).

1 Corinthians 9:19-22 (MSG) – "Even though I am free of the demands and expectations of everyone, I have voluntarily become a servant to any and all in order to reach a wide range of people: religious, nonreligious, meticulous moralists, loose-living immoralists, the defeated, the demoralized—whoever. I didn't take on their way of life. I kept my bearings in Christ—but I entered their world and tried to experience things from their point of view. I've become just about every sort of servant there is in my attempts to lead those I meet into a God-saved life."

The Apostle Paul, in his selflessness, sacrificed what he could've done so that he could reach those who he was called to for Jesus. He entered into their world and experienced things from their point of view. He did this so he could relate to who he was called to serve, which made him relatable. He did this without compromising his convictions for God and breaking God's law to connect with everyone and win them to Christ. The Apostle Paul was free of other people's opinions about him, but for the sake of his assignment, he thought enough about other opinions and their view of him so he could win them to Christ. It's dangerous for a person with great influence to say, "I don't care what people think about me. "While man's aim should be to please God, man should always be mindful that their actions (not always sinful actions) can cause them to be less effective towards a certain group of people. The Apostle Paul told the church at Corinth in 1 Corinthians 10:23 (TPT) that, *"you all say, "we're allowed to do anything we choose" (under grace) but not everything causes the spiritual advancement of others."* Nehemiah was governor of Judah for 12 years. 12 is the number of government and order. Nehemiah's 12-year reign was significant of the reality that God placed him in that governmental system of Judah to bring order, structure, and government to that government. In past times, some of the governors that were reigning in Judah were not bringing structure but were rather creating cultures of oppression.

The Lord is raising up Nehemiahs because of their selflessness to deal with injustice that has been perpetrated but not exposed within governmental places. They have called to confront systems of oppression. In this new era, the world will experience and see great shaking. Systems of oppression will be broken so that people can live the way God wants them to live-without unnecessary hardship. Systems of oppression will be exposed and evicted. In Nehemiah Chapter 5, the creditors of the land of Judah and those who worked in the money systems were operating illegally and unfairly against the people of the land. Nehemiah 5:12-13 (KJV), *"Then said they, We will restore them, and will require nothing of them; so will we do as thou sayest. Then I called the priests, and took an oath of them, that they should do according to this promise. 13 Also I shook my lap, and said, So God shake out every man from his house, and from his labour, that performeth not this promise, even thus be he shaken out, and emptied. And all the congregation said, Amen, and praised the Lord. And the people did according to this promise."*

The Lord spoke to me in January 2023 and said that there will be a political uproar in the United States.

Nehemiah said that God would shake personal possessions out of the hands of those who don't keep their vows. This has already begun: however, another wave greater than what has already transpired will take place in governments. There is coming a great shaking to governments in America and all around the globe in the political arena. We will see people removed from offices and positions who have intentionally created and continued systems of bondage that have oppressed people for so long. We will see the Lord raise up leaders who, with apostolic and prophetic authority, will implement laws and systems that will cause people to no longer be oppressed. This shaking will provoke wealth transfers. Wealth transfers will transpire under the leadership of emerging Nehemiahs while they are functioning as both prophetic voices in the Kingdom and as governmental gatekeepers. Where would the possessions that Nehemiah said that God would shake out of the hands of those that don't keep their vows go? Proverbs 13:22 (CEV) says, *"If you obey God, you will have something to leave your grandchildren. If you don't obey God, those who live right will get what you leave."*

Those who have been living right will experience this wealth transfer. This is one of the reasons why governmental gatekeepers are important and why God plants them in government systems that need to be shaken or that He's getting ready to shake. God uses a voice to declare where He's getting ready to shake. Whenever governments experience shaking and exposure, it is an indication that a wealth transfer is currently or about to happen. There is also great restoration happening in the body of Christ right now. We will begin to see the introduction to the great restoration and restitution. Restoration deals God's giving people what they lost. Restitution deals with God giving His people what they would've had if they had not suffered loss at all. The restoration that transpired in Nehemiah Chapter 5 involved everything that had been taken from the children of Israel being given back all at once, including the interest they had been charged. In the great restoration that is happening now according to Nehemiah 5:11 (GNT), which says, *"Cancel all the debts they owe you—money or grain or wine or olive oil. And give them back their fields, vineyards, olive groves, and houses right now!"* I believe everything is coming now and all at one time.

Nehemiah's selflessness opened a door for those who worked with him to become the people who sat with him. Nehemiah became more intimate with those who he served and who served alongside him. This is the kind of Kingdom people who are arising, those who are genuinely concerned about people. I'm sure as these people sat down at Nehemiah's table, they asked him questions and voiced their concerns, as they had access to the powerful and prominent leader. Jesus was this kind of leader. His apostles sat down with him in intimate settings. In those settings, He allowed them to ask Him questions. He also poured into them spiritually and fed them when they became physically hungry. People will always want to sit with and learn from those who know how to progress. I'm also sure that the people who sat with Nehemiah at his table saw how he treated people and how kind he was to others. Nehemiah brought order and confronted economic injustice as governor while still continuing to build the wall. Nehemiah 5:16 (KJV), *"Yea, also I continued in the work of this wall."* Nehemiah had different graces upon his life to accomplish different tasks. He was graced to be a prophetic voice and apostolic leader to a nation and had to build, fight, galvanize, and function in government all at once. Those graces were functioning and operating at one time. Nehemiah multitasked and was able to focus while doing so. Emerging Nehemiahs will have the grace to aggregate and balance many different tasks because of the demand from the Kingdom of God. They will not experience burnout while balancing multiple tasks at once because of the grace of God. Burnout is, but is not limited to, when one becomes devoid of energy and physically and mentally drained. The Apostle Paul said in 1 Corinthians 16:10 (NLT), *"For I have worked harder than any of the other apostles; yet it was not I but God who was working through me by his grace."* He was cognizant of the grace of God enabling him to do what he did. When Nehemiah came from the palace at Shushan to Judah and Jerusalem, he came fully available and ready to be used by God. This is a prophetic paradigm that when you give God your all, He will give you His all and trust you with more. Emerging Nehemiahs will be multidimensional and multifaceted, which will make them effective in their endeavors. It's never the will of God for any of His children to live a one-dimensional life. To be one-dimensional is to stay on one level and never ascend to a higher level of living, including while functioning in your assignment.

In Nehemiah 5:5, Nehemiah confronted a culture that currently on the mind of God, and he's confronting it now. The bible says in Nehemiah 5:5 (KJV), *"Yet now our flesh is as the flesh of our brethren, our children as their children: and, lo, we bring into bondage our sons and our daughters to be servants, and some of our daughters are brought unto bondage already: neither is it in our power to redeem them; for other men have our lands and vineyards."* In Nehemiah's time, the children were being robbed of their childhood because they had to work as adults due to the system of oppression in place. Their parents had to recruit them to make ends meet. In contemporary terms, these children had to get after-school and weekend jobs to help their parents pay bills. Therefore, before they could get started with life, they were pulled into adult responsibilities. God is, in this era, breaking this cycle of bondage so that children can maximize the opportunities available to them as children and focus on the future. The times in the world are getting darker, but God's people will live in Goshen. Children who've been raised in impoverished conditions and that have been forced into bondage will no longer be subjected to bondage. Nehemiahs will implement changes that will allow every generation to be better.

Two-Fold In The Assignment (Watch & Fight, Work & Build)

Nehemiah 4:13-22 (KJV)

[13] *Therefore set I in the lower places behind the wall, and on the higher places, I even set the people after their families with their swords, their spears, and their bows.*

[14] *And I looked, and rose up, and said unto the nobles, and to the rulers, and to the rest of the people, Be not ye afraid of them: remember the Lord, which is great and terrible, and fight for your brethren, your sons, and your daughters, your wives, and your houses.*

[15] *And it came to pass, when our enemies heard that it was known unto us, and God had brought their counsel to nought, that we returned all of us to the wall, every one unto his work.*

[16] *And it came to pass from that time forth, that the half of my servants wrought in the work, and the other half of them held both the spears, the shields, and the bows, and the habergeons; and the rulers were behind all the house of Judah.*

[17] They which builded on the wall, and they that bare burdens, with those that laded, every one with one of his hands wrought in the work, and with the other hand held a weapon.

[18] For the builders, every one had his sword girded by his side, and so builded. And he that sounded the trumpet was by me.

[19] And I said unto the nobles, and to the rulers, and to the rest of the people, The work is great and large, and we are separated upon the wall, one far from another.

[20] In what place therefore ye hear the sound of the trumpet, resort ye thither unto us: our God shall fight for us.

[21] So we laboured in the work: and half of them held the spears from the rising of the morning till the stars appeared.

[22] Likewise at the same time said I unto the people, Let every one with his servant lodge within Jerusalem, that in the night they may be a guard to us, and labour on the day.

[23] So neither I, nor my brethren, nor my servants, nor the men of the guard which followed me, none of us put off our clothes, saving that every one put them off for washing.

We are living in a time where builders must now be two-fold in their assignment. The enemy has turned up the thermostat of warfare against the body of Christ. Daniel 3:19 (KJV) says, *"Then when was Nebuchadnezzar full of fury, and the form of his visage was changed against Shadrach, Meshach, and Abednego: therefore he spake, and commanded that they should heat the furnace one seven times more than it was wont to be heated."* Nebuchadnezzar spoke and commanded that the furnace be turned up seven times hotter. When warfare increases, guarding must increase. The Body of Christ should never be reactive to the kingdom of darkness but proactive. Nehemiah put men on the wall, and they were building with a tool in one hand and a weapon in the other. They had to be on alert and on guard regarding their enemies. They were moving with urgency because of the magnitude of the time and their assignment. There is a remnant in the earth that will be just as engaged spiritually on how to war and deal with warfare as they are naturally skilled and alert. They will know how to combat the forces of darkness. In Nehemiah 4:12, there were Jews who dwelt close enough to Nehemiah's adversaries that they were able to report and expose their moves. The Bible said that the Jews did this ten times. Ten is the number of completion. This means that the Lord began to completely expose what was transpiring and being planned. The Lord will not allow His people to fight blindly, missing the target and not hitting the mark. Emerging Nehemiahs will know exactly what to pray and intercede against because of the revelation and insight that they receive so that they can war effectively, strategically, and successfully. In 2 Kings 6, the King of Syria was attempting to war against Israel and was drawing up a strategy, but everything he tried to do was exposed because the Lord would reveal it to Elisha, the prophet. This is what the Lord is doing. He is revealing to His prophets and people what they need to know to have the advantage that we need. God is planting His people in systems and places to hear the demonic agendas that are being created so that they can be prayed against and contested in various ways.

Nehemiah 4:13 (KJV) – "Therefore set I in the lower places behind the wall, and on the higher places, I even set the people after their families with their swords, their spears, and their bows."

The low places were the places that the enemy would be most likely to attack because they weren't elevated and built. It was a bare place where there was an opening. The enemy attacks individuals in their lives and assignments where he sees an opening. It doesn't always have to be big things. Sometimes it's the small things and doors that give the enemy access to disrupt everything. Songs of Solomon 2:15 says, *"Catch the foxes for us, the little foxes that spoil the vineyards, for our vineyards are in blossom."* When a man is walking in their assignment, they must make sure not to leave any place unguarded because any door left open gives the enemy access. Examples of a low place for one could be feeling inadequate, having low self-esteem, feelings of rejection, or even being easily offended; the enemy attacks when these and many other feelings are present in people. In general, especially in one's personal life, a low place can be just that, a low place in one's life. A place where it looks like life isn't working out, and everything is falling apart. If one doesn't keep momentum in this place, they will lose ground and give the enemy the upper hand. A low place can be a place of unrepented sin where the enemy can capitalize off of fear, unbelief, insecurity, a love for money, or pride. It can also be past issues that are affecting the present, such as future relationships and every area of a man's life. A low place can also be translated as a hard or difficult place.

High places were places where those who were stationed there could see their enemy and events coming from a distance. I believe Nehemiah was intentional about who he set in this high place, because he was a man led by God. The higher you ascend, the more you see. One has to be able to see to be in this place. The elevation that one receives in the natural should only be an indication of what has already happened in the Spirit. Everybody can't be set up in the high places naturally because they can't see well enough spiritually to occupy that position. If one has a lack of vision, they lack ascension. The men in the high place on the wall knew what enemies they had to be on guard for. Had they not known what to be on the watch for, then Sanballat, Tobiah, and Geshem could've come close to the wall and attacked. Ascension is important, because sometimes it's not that people don't know how to war effectively; it's that people at times don't know what to war against. This is one of the reasons why God supernaturally takes His people into the future in the spirit realm and allows us to see visions concerning what the enemy is planning. Isaiah 21:6 (KJV), *"For thus hath the Lord said unto me, Go, set a watchman, let him declare what he seeth."* Seers and those stationed on walls who see over families or regions are so vital, as they declare what they have seen. God wants His people to see ahead of time what's coming, as these men in the high places on the wall in the book of Nehemiah could see. Your vision is an important factor in contributing to your victory. We as the body of Christ should have a greater desire to see further than even where we may see now.

Let's pray this prayer together right now. "Father, I thank you that you are sharpening my vision through the person of the Holy Spirit. Let me see with clarity, precision, and accuracy. Thank you, Father, that as you asked the Prophet Jeremiah, "What do you see, Jeremiah?" Lord, you were training his vision. Thank you that you are likewise training my vision, to see and to know when I've seen what you've shown me and when you have not shown me what I think you may have shown me. Lord, you then told the Prophet Jeremiah that "thou has seen well." Thank you that I see well, now, in Jesus name. May as the Apostle Paul when he was praying for the church at Ephesus in Ephesians 1, said, "that the eyes of your understanding being enlightened." Thank you, Father, that the eyes of my understanding are enlightened that I may know what the hope of his calling is and what the riches of the glory of his inheritance in the saints. I cover my eye gate in the natural in Jesus name, so that it doesn't affect my ability to see in the spirit realm. Thank you, Father, that as Elisha prayed for his servant that you would open his eyes that he may see and you opened the servant's eyes. I'm asking you, now, to open my eyes spiritually so that I may see, and as you did it for Elisha the Prophet's servant you are doing it for me. I have a better covenant than those of the Old Testament had, and it's established upon better promises. Lord, I pray that I would see further. Thank you, Father, that I see clearly in dreams and visions in Jesus name I pray Amen."

(I even set the people after their families with their)

Those stationed in low and high places have been equipped with swords as they engage in their assignment as watchmen. Swords are objects that have a sharp ending on their side or sides that's meant to cut, kill, and destroy. The body of Christ is living in a time where it is imperative that one uses their sword like never before. In Ephesians 6:17 (KJV), the Apostle Paul tells the church at Ephesus, *"And take the helmet of salvation, and the sword of the Spirit, which is the word of God."* Every believer has been equipped with the sword of the Spirit. You've been given a sword and authority to do damage to the kingdom of darkness. You have authority to destroy, in the spirit realm, everything that has been attacking and will attempt to attack what Apostle Dannie Williams calls "the 5 pillars of your life." These "5 pillars" include your spiritual, physical, emotional, financial, and educational well-being. Believers must use their sword to cut off and destroy everything that is designed to keep them from being spiritually healthy and progressing. The enemy will attempt to attack every person's physical well-being with sickness. You must however, use your sword, which is the word of the God, and confess and receive your healing according to Matthew 8:17 (KJV), which says, *"Himself took our infirmities, and bare our sicknesses."* Emotional trauma and pain will hinder people from fulfilling purpose and walking in destiny. The enemy is using the emotional wounds of people as leverage to keep them in bondage and to destroy them.

Believers must use their sword to cut off, destroy, and deal with what will destroy their emotional well-being. Psalms 112:3 (KJV) says, *"Wealth and riches shall be in his house: and his righteousness endureth for ever."* This shows that it is the will of God for believers to be financially wealthy. According to Galatians 3:13 (KJV), *"Christ has redeemed us from the curse of the law, being made a curse for us…"* Deuteronomy 28:45-48 identifies one of the curses as poverty. Therefore, when poverty is manifesting, and a believer knows they're walking in obedience, they must use their sword to cut off and destroy poverty from their life. Education is not mandatory, nonetheless important. If the enemy can fight against you in this area and stop you from advancing educationally to gain knowledge that will propel your life, he will. The 5 pillars on the other side of getting victory in these 5 areas is being biblically responsible and practical. Take responsibility for your spiritual well-being by being intentional. You do this by reading the word of God, praying, worshiping, and practicing intimacy with the Holy Spirit. It is also important that one be a doer of the Word which causes spiritual growth. Take responsibility for your physical well-being. Eat healthily and constantly examine your spiritual and physical life to protect your physical well-being. Unforgiveness, bitterness, and not discerning the Lord's body are reasons why one can be sick because of not being spiritually responsible. Accept accountability for your financial well-being by spending your money wisely and by following biblical principles. We must deal with emotional trauma and reach out for assistance to maintain deliverance. Don't allow the devil to rob you of your transformation through crafty tactics. Accept accountability for your educational well-being. Be intentional about educating yourself and receiving knowledge that will cause you to be better in life. The Apostle Paul was intentional about his educational well-being being in great condition. In 2 Timothy 4:13 (NLT), the Apostle Paul told Timothy, *"When you come, be sure to bring the coat I left with Carpus at Troas. Also bring my books, and especially my papers."* This means that the Apostle Paul was a reader of books. He was intentional about gaining knowledge.

The next point I would like to discuss is the concept of utilizing your spear. Those who have been as watchmen have been equipped with spears. A spear is a doubled-edged sharp object that can be thrown and is used for piercing and breaking through. God has given His people spears of authority to break through places spiritually to get victory in every area of our lives. Most times when the story is told about David and Goliath, it's told from the perspective of a young, smaller, and anointed David killing a giant Philistine giant. That's a great way to explain the story because it's true. It is also however significant because of David breaking through a place that others (the warriors of Israel, including David's brothers) struggled to break through and get victory in. You who are reading this will be the David that breaks through and gets breakthroughs in areas that others have struggled to get victory in or didn't get the victory in. It doesn't matter who didn't get over the hump! It doesn't matter how many people it affected generationally! It doesn't matter how many people have suffered with and from it! It doesn't matter how many people it happened to! God has equipped you with a spear to pierce through to a place, even if you're the first one to ever do it.

The bow is a weapon used from long range to strike. It is also spiritually significant of a doctrine of truth according to Isaiah 5:28 and Habakkuk 3:9, and arrows are truths from the truth. Isaiah 5:28 (KJV), *"Whose arrows are sharp, and all their bows bent, their horses' hoofs shall be counted like flint, and their wheels like a whirlwind."* Habakkuk 3:9 (KJV), *"Thy bow was made quite naked, according to the oaths of the tribes, even thy word. Selah. Thou didst cleave the earth with rivers."* God has equipped His people with bows. We must shoot the bow that we have been armed with, which is God's truth, into situations, circumstances, and at the enemy to change what needs to be changed. Truth will prevail, and every lie will be exposed. The scripture teaches us in Romans 3:4 (KJV), *"God forbid: yea, let God be true, but every man a liar; as it is written, That thou mightest be justified in thy sayings, and mightest overcome when thou art judged."* As believers and watchmen, we carry bows, which is truth. Truth is needed in this time that the world is in. We must declare what God has declared over our lives despite what we may be faced with. As bows reach a long range, God has given us bows to go back into the past spiritually and shut down demonic portals, generational curses, and all ungodly activity. With this bow that we have been equipped with, we have also been given authority to go into the future spiritually with truth and declare what will and won't manifest.

The bow that God has equipped His church with can reach where we can't go physically, but as spiritual beings, we can reach into a place in the spirit realm and obtain what God has ordained for us. For those who will use their bow, they will not be caught off guard because they are in the low and high places to stop what's happening there. One must responsibly carry a bow because, as truth from the word of God can be used to bless, it can also be used to manipulate. We must use the bows that God has given to speak what God has declared in His word for that moment. This must be done with pure motives, with no other purpose but to be obedient to the will of God and see people's lives better. Nehemiah 4:14 (KJV), *"And I looked, and rose up, and said unto the nobles, and to the rulers, and to the rest of the people, Be not ye afraid of them: remember the Lord, which is great and terrible, and fight for your brethren, your sons, and your daughters, your wives, and your houses."* Nehemiah wasn't so concerned about his assignment that he neglected to tell the men about the importance of their assignment to their families. He told them to *"fight for your brethren, your sons, and your daughters, your wives, and your houses."*

He was, in other words, telling them not to leave any doors open in their houses or families but to cover and protect their families in all aspects. Emerging Nehemiahs will be those who know not only the importance of people to function in their Kingdom assignment but also how important it is for their houses to be in order and covered. This is what an apostolic leader does. They not only pour into you concerning the spiritual aspect but also the practical side of life as well. This is because it is not the will of God for men or leaders in families (if there's no man present) to function in their Kingdom assignment while their families fall apart and are left uncovered. The first ministry is the family ministry. Marriage was the first institution that God established in the earth, and it was established long before the church was. When God established the church, it was because of sin and people needing to be saved, but when He established marriage, it was because of covenant. Covenant is a direct reflection of God. Therefore, the thing that God established in the earth first speaks to the beginning order of how God prioritizes.

One of the signs that a person is not an emerging Nehemiah is if they only speak to you about your purpose but never provoke people to be better husbands, wives, and children. In this scripture, Nehemiah was speaking of physically covering; however, a man must also cover his family spiritually through prayer. Nehemiah didn't address the women and say, "fight for," he told the men. Therefore, a man should be the lead prayer warrior in his home. In today's society, there is a great need for men and fathers to be present in the home. Statistics state that when a father is present in the home, a girl is less likely to get pregnant early on, and a boy is more likely to stay out of trouble because of the father's presence. The Lord, in these last days, is causing the family dynamic to return to the way that He always intended for it to be. Nehemiah didn't, nor was he attempting to raise up a bunch of men who were hard workers but absent family men. One should never be so busy that they can't attend to your household. What good would it have been if the wall was built, but their families died from attacks and their houses were destroyed? What good is it if one fulfills their Kingdom assignment while their house is left uncovered and eventually torn apart? The Bible in Nehemiah 4:14 is showing and teaching us how a man should respond when life gets challenging and difficult and when attacks are coming against his house. That is to cover his family like never before. This also shows that while man is attending to one area of life, the enemy will try to attack another area. Life was indeed happening at the beginning of the book of Nehemiah, meaning what Jesus said in John 16:33 (KJV), *"In the world ye shall have tribulation,"* they were in a crisis. However, Nehemiah said to "fight for." A man should always fight for and never against his family. They should never allow what life throws at them to cause them to take it out on their family. Vice versa as well from a wife to a husband. Family is so important to God that the last verse in the Old Testament speaks on the family dynamic and what God will do through the spirit of Elijah in the earth. At the beginning of the book of Nehemiah, Nehemiah said "let us build so that we are no longer a reproach." After Nehemiah began to function in the land of Judah and Jerusalem, they were no longer a reproach. Not just because they built the walls and other nations saw it. It was also because God was pleased with Nehemiah raising up not only men who were great builders and warriors but also attentive fathers, husbands, and family members. Proverbs 22:1 (KJV), *"A good name is rather to be chosen than great riches."* God wants it to be said of his men that they are excellent husbands and fathers and great family members. Believers are a direct reflection of God in the eyes of the world. Therefore, if husbands and fathers are neglectful, then we become a reproach to the world. A sign of Nehemiah's era is that godly fathers and husbands will be on display, demonstrating the principles of God as they walk in the covenant with God. Nehemiah 7:3 (NASB), *"Then I said* to them, *"The gates of Jerusalem are not to be opened until the sun is hot, and while they are standing guard, the gatekeepers are to keep the doors shut and bolted."* Also *"appoint guards from the inhabitants of Jerusalem, each at his post, and each in front of his own house."* After the wall was built and work was completed, Nehemiah still emphasized the importance of men being stationed in front of their homes and appointed them as such. Nehemiah 8:13 (NIV), *"On the second day of the month, the heads of all the families, along with the priests and the Levites, gathered around Ezra the teacher to give attention to the words of the Law."* These same men and fathers that Nehemiah provoked and challenged to fight for their families gave attention to the word of God that Ezra was teaching in Nehemiah 8:13. They then brought what they learned home to their families and houses and caused them to understand it. This shows that it is not solely the preacher's or the pastor's responsibility but the head of the house's responsibility. The man is the priest and the prophet of his household. He is responsible for leading his family spiritually. Nehemiah 4:22 (KJV), *"Likewise at the same time said I unto the people, Let every one with his servant lodge within Jerusalem, that in the night they may be a guard to us, and labour on the day."* Nehemiah understood the importance of nighttime guards because of the activity that can and does transpire at night. In a time where there's so much activity transpiring in the realm of the Spirit, the nighttime guards, who are intercessors, are important. Intercessors through prayer and intercession prohibit events from happening. This is one of the reasons why God has intercessors up in the late hours of the night and early hours of the morning. Those are hours when a lot of demonic activity transpires but are also hours when people of God can pray and tap into the presence of God with ease. The builders, guards, and servants in Nehemiah 4:22 didn't live in Jerusalem but outside of the city. Nehemiah called the builders, guards, and servants to stay in the place where they were building. They were all in and didn't leave. Intercessors don't have permission to abandon the place of their assignment and then come back. They are full-time watchmen and guards who are never off guard. I'm sure these guards, servers, and builders had families that they were away from while lodging at Jerusalem. They paid a cost to guard at night. Intercessors pay with their lives to protect other people. Not in the sense of physical death, but they die to their will to protect and guard. These same nighttime guards were builders in the daytime. Intercessors build up standards of protection through prayer and then guard it against illegal activity. God also never called intercessors to be lazy in the physical. They are active people who work during the day, sometimes on secular jobs while they guard.

Refresh, Don't Relax

Nehemiah 4:23 (NLT) – "During this time, none of us—not I, nor my relatives, nor my servants, nor the guards who were with me—ever took off our clothes. We carried our weapons with us at all times, even when we went for water."

We are in a season and living in a time when you can't afford to disarm yourself at any time, even in moments of refreshing. When Nehemiah, his relatives, servants, and the guards would go to bathe, they wouldn't take their clothes off or disarm themselves of their weapons. This is symbolic of them not removing what kept them safe from their enemies. They understood how important their weapons were to them. The weapons that they didn't disarm themselves of were physical, but for the New Testament believer, the Bible teaches in 2 Corinthians 10:4-5 (KJV), *"4 (For the weapons of our warfare are not carnal, but mighty through God to the pulling down of strong holds;) 5 Casting down imaginations, and every high thing that exalteth itself against the knowledge of God, and bringing into captivity every thought to the obedience of Christ."* Believers don't fight naturally and physically but in the spirit realm. Fighting in the spirit may at times require physical actions but battles are won in the realm of the spirit. Nehemiah was a man of prayer and knew firsthand that battles are won in prayer and fasting. What manifests in the natural is only an indication of what has been done or labored for in the spirit realm.

Nehemiah started praying and fasting in the month of "Chisleu" and didn't stop until the month of "Nisan." When the answer to his prayer manifested and the king asked, "what would you have me to do for you?" That's a span of 4 months. In scripture, the children of Israel didn't stop fasting until they got the answer as to why they began to fast in the first place or until they saw victory. Even Daniel in Daniel chapter 10 didn't stop fasting until he received clear direction and the answer to the purpose of his fast. It took Nehemiah and the builders less than 2 months to build the wall, 52 days, while he prayed and fasted for 4 months. Nehemiah's time of consecration was longer than the building of the wall. This shows us a majority of a prophet's ministry activity is behind the scenes and a smaller portion is in public. When believers relax and shift into autopilot mode spiritually, we stop pursuing what God has given us a license to pursue. We stop guarding who, what, and where God has given us authority and jurisdiction to guard. Yes, believers should rest in the finished work of Jesus Christ on the cross. The finished work of Jesus Christ has brought man into a place of victory through grace if they accept it. However, believers still have a responsibility to guard and remain on guard. Their bathing in water is symbolic of spiritual and physical refreshing, with water being a type of the Spirit. The Bible tells in Acts 3:19 that times of refreshing come from the presence of the Lord. The act of not removing their clothes while bathing meant that they didn't remove their covering or disconnect from what covered them.

The enemy is waiting for you to slip, because according to 1 Peter 5:8, *"Satan, walketh about, seeking whom he may devour."* How does one step outside of the covering of the Lord? One way is when we begin to operate in rebellion against God and through stubbornness. 1 Samuel 15:23 teaches that, *"rebellion is as the sin of witchcraft, and stubbornness is as iniquity and idolatry."* This is what the Prophet Samuel told King Saul after he rebelled against God and was stubborn concerning what the Prophet Samuel told him. From there we see the downward spiral of Saul's life. 1 Samuel 16:23 (KJV) then says something very important relative to covering, *"But the Spirit of the LORD departed from Saul, and an evil spirit from the LORD troubled him."* A better way to articulate this would be that God allowed an evil spirit to come upon Saul because nothing about God is evil therefore; He doesn't have an evil spirit to send. After Saul's rebellion and stubbornness, the Spirit of the Lord, which came upon

Saul to complete the work that he had been raised up to do, left him. That left an opening for an evil spirit to come in. The prophetic paradigm of this is that when we step outside of the covering of the Lord, we automatically subject ourselves to the forces of darkness and all that comes along with it. When men are stubborn, they are inviting demonic activity into their lives. Wise counsel keeps us safe and covered. Proverbs 16:18 (KJV) says, *"Pride goeth before destruction, and an haughty spirit before a fall."* Lucifer fell from his place in heaven because of pride, and the Bible said that iniquity was found in him (Ezekiel 28:15). The seed of stubbornness will produce the same harvest as it produced for Lucifer. Those who are stubborn operate in idolatry, making it about them. Isaiah 14:12-13 (KJV) says, *"For thou hast said in thine heart, I will ascend into heaven, I will exalt my throne above the stars of God: I will sit also upon the mount of the congregation, in the sides of the north: 14 I will ascend above the heights of the clouds; I will be like the most High."* The 5 I's that Lucifer declared was idolatry. Idolatry causes man to focus on who they are and what they want rather than who God is and what He wants. There is no more safety, as there was none for Lucifer. There is safety in God's best. Love is also a weapon against the enemy because if we stay and walk in love, we can always be assured that our prayers will not be hindered.

It's important to know that refreshing doesn't involve stopping; it's where you get more zeal so that you won't stop. Nehemiahs will know when refreshing is needed but will not take it as an opportunity to relax. The kingdom of darkness never stops working. As a matter of fact, in the natural world we may say, "The devil is working overtime." So much activity is happening; there are wars, rumors of wars, nations against nations, and kingdom against kingdom, famines, and earthquakes in diverse places. There is no time to relax in a time of war when such ferocious events are happening. The times are intense, so the people of God must be also. The body of Christ can't afford to relax.

Sound

Hearing and Releasing the Sound

Nehemiah 4:20 (NKJV) – "Wherever you hear the sound of the trumpet, rally to us there. Our God will fight for us."

The word sound in Hebrew is "qol," which means "voice". (Biblehub.com) Protection in this season and era will come through being sensitive to the sound of heaven and the voice of the Lord. Sound will be a huge factor for victory. The sound that God is releasing from heaven into the earth is vital for direction, even as the Lord told David not to move until he heard the sound of the mulberry tree. Nehemiah instructed the builders and watchmen that wherever they hear the sound of the trumpet, rally there, for the Lord will fight for them. This is symbolic of God speaking and moving in a specific place and His people having to be in a position to hear. God is not going to change the location of where His sound comes from; therefore, we must change our location to come close to Him. Jeremiah 23:18 (KJV) says, *"For who hath stood in the counsel of the LORD, and hath perceived and heard his word? who hath marked his word, and heard it?"* This shows us that God speaks from a specific place or places, and man must change their location by ascending into the counsel of God to hear the sound and voice of the Lord.

God releases sound in a moment, and not being acquainted with the sound of the Lord could cost you. Nehemiah informed the people of the sound that would be heard before something happened; therefore, people had no excuse not to respond when it sounded. Nehemiah didn't say "if you hear the sound of the trumpet", he said when. For those who didn't know what the trumpet sounded like, they had time prior to it being sounded to become acquainted with it. We are in a time when God is giving His people an opportunity to be acquainted with His sound, His voice, and other ways that He's sounding alarms. God will release a sound that will cause His will in the earth and for His people's lives to come to pass. Sound is an indicator that God is moving, speaking, or giving direction for His people. When God releases a sound, it's an indication the heaven's forecast is manifesting. It's a way to follow His mind. This is the reason why it's important for those that have ears to hear what the Spirit is saying unto the church because merely having ears isn't an indication of hearing correctly. Jeremiah 5:21 (NIV) says, *"Hear this, you foolish and senseless people who have eyes but do not see, and have ears but do hear."* Foolish people choose not to hear and become acquainted with what's being released that's vital for them to hear. Sound gets people's attention. In traffic, a car horn is utilized to draw someone's attention. The sound of the horn causes them to look and find out what was happening or what provoked them to blow it. Sound makes people curious. Have you ever heard a loud noise and been curious to find out what it was and where it came from? In scripture, the trumpet was used to indicate what is happening. Trumpet in Hebrew is the word "shophar." (Biblehub.com) A shofar is a ram's horn, which is very loud. Prophets in the Old Testament would blow the shofar to indicate the time. The word "shofar" originates from the word "shaphar," which means "to be beautiful." Everything that God does is in and out of love, so I believe that the end result of God releasing sound is to make things beautiful in the end.

Ecclesiastes 3:11 (KJV) – "He hath made Everything beautiful in his time: Also he hath sent the world in their heart, So that no man can find out the work that God make it from the beginning to the end."

God uses different sounds in diverse ways. He releases sound that can be heard from the counsel of the heavens; the sound that God releases comes out of eternity. When Jesus comes back to rapture the church, there will be sounds released.

1 Thessalonians 4:16 (KJV) – "For the Lord himself sound sent from heaven with a shout and with the voice of the archangel, and with the trump of God and the dead in Christ shall rise first."

Jesus Himself shall release a sound on that day. One translation says Jesus shall release "a cry of command," which means "sound commands". The archangel shall release a sound, and with the trumpet of God.

John, the revelator, saw and recorded in the book of Revelation that there will be seven angels with seven trumpets sounding them as God released judgment during the tribulation (between Revelation chapters 8 and 11). Another example would be, before Elijah or his servant saw rain, Elijah heard it. Elijah told King Ahab in 1 Kings 18:41, *"Get thee up, eat and drink; for there is a sound of abundance of rain."* How do you suppose he heard it? He had to hear it supernaturally by the Spirit of God in the realm of the spirit. The sound that Elijah heard was the indicator to give direction to King Ahab about what to do. He then told his servant to go and check for rain because he knew what was coming based on the sound that came out of eternity. After his servant told him that he saw a cloud the size of a man's hand, he told his servant to tell Ahab to prepare his chariot and get ready for the rain. Sound should always birth or provoke movement. Elijah then girded his loins and ran ahead of Ahab's horse to Jezreel. A sound produced and provoked movement. When God came down to meet with the children of Israel on Mount Sinai, there was a sound released. Exodus 19:19 (KJV) says, *"And when the voice of the trumpet sounded long, and waxed louder and louder, Moses spoke, and God answered him by a voice."* The closer God came to the children on the mountain, the louder the trumpet sounded. There wasn't a man playing the trumpet; this came out of heaven. The prophetic paradigm of this is that the closer we get to God, the louder the sound of the Lord becomes to us. We, as God's people, can determine the level of intimacy based on the volume of the Lord that He releases to us. Even as God releases sound to His people, His people release sound in the earth.

Man must make sure that their sound doesn't become distorted, or else it becomes ineffective. When the Apostle Paul in 1 Corinthians 14 is explaining tongues and its function, he asks a profound question in verse 8, *"If the trumpet, which is man, give off an uncertain sound…,"* which is whatever is releasing out of their mouth, *"who shall himself prepare for battle?"* meaning who shall get in position to prepare for what is happening. The word that is uncertain in the King James is translated in the original text as indistinct, which is the word "adelos" in the Greek. (Bibletools.org) Adelos in Greek means "unseen, not obvious, inconspicuous, or indistinct". This is the reason why it's crucial that man allow God to birth an authentic sound in the spirits. This sound comes through intimacy with and yielding to the Holy Spirit. An uncertain sound doesn't mean that what the person is releasing or saying is wrong or that the timing in which they are releasing it is wrong. It means that the sound isn't recognizable enough to fulfill its purpose because it's off. When the day of Pentecost fully came in Acts chapter 2, there was a sound as of a rushing mighty wind released from heaven. Rushing, mighty, and wind are significant in themselves as they all relate to sound.

The word rushing in Greek is the word "pheró," which means "to bear, carry, or bring forth". (Biblehub.com) Whenever God releases a sound, it is indicative of a reality that God is ushering in and bringing forth a move of the Spirit; He uses a sound that carries to do it. The word mighty in the original text is the word violent. This word violent in Greek means "biaios," which comes from "bia" which means "force, violence, and strength". (Biblehub.com) Whenever God releases sound, there is enough force in the frequency for the sound to move everything in its path. Psalms 62:11 (KJV) says, *"God hath spoken once; twice have I heard this; that power belongeth unto God."* The psalmist heard what God spoke twice even though He said it once because of the force in the sound that carried it. Whenever God speaks, man is left with no choice but to listen because of the force attached to His sound. This is also why it is imperative to protect the purity of the sound of worship and music because the force in it allows whoever is hearing it to receive from God. The word "wind" in Greek is "pnoé," which means "a blowing wind or breath". (Biblehub.com) Whenever God releases sound, He's releasing His breath. God's breath has life in it. Whenever the Lord releases a sound, He's releasing His life into a person, situation, or atmosphere to cause a shift. Genesis 2:7 (KJV) says, *"And the LORD God formed man of the dust of the ground, and breathed into his nostrils the breath of life; and man became a living soul."* One of the purposes of sound is to release life to where there is death. This is why at the sound of the trumpet, the dead in Christ shall rise first. They shall rise at a sound.

Nehemiah 12:43 (NIV) – *"And on that day they offered great sacrifices, rejoicing because God had given them great joy. The women and children also rejoiced. The sound of rejoicing in Jerusalem could be heard far away."*

We have entered an era where man will no longer know preachers by their sermons but by their sound. Man will no longer know worship leaders by their song but by their sound. Man will no longer know intercessors by their secrets but by the sound that they release. Everybody has a word, but whose sound will cause things to come into alignment? Why do people require more than a sermon, song, or a secret? It's because in a culture where everybody is preaching the same sermon, singing the same song, or declaring the same secret, then no one is different and distinct. You are distinguished by your sound. The sound that you release and that you carry distinguishes you. James and John were referred to as the sons of thunder, which means that they came from and carried a sound that shook everything. I believe in this era, the James and Johns are getting ready to emerge, and they carry a powerful sound. Jesus gave His apostles and disciples the same assignment when He sent them out into different regions. However, we know that James and John carried a sound of thunder that roared and caused a shift where they were. The Greek word for "thunder" in Mark 3:17 is the word "bronté," which means "to roar". (Biblehub.com) The word bronté is translated 12 times in the New Testament. Each of those 12 times, this word is used in relation to or referring to a sound that sounded like thunder or thunder itself. In John 12:29, when the Father spoke in an audible voice from Heaven to Jesus for the people's sake, some said that it was thunder. Therefore, when you carry thunder, you are carrying the sound of God. One of the twelve times the word bronté is translated in the New Testament is in Revelation 10:4. Revelation 10:4 gives great insight as to what this sound is and what it does. Revelation 10:4 (KJV) says, *"And when the seven thunders had uttered their voices, I was about to write: and I heard a voice from heaven saying unto me, Seal up those things which the seven thunders uttered, and write them not."* This scripture doesn't say man spoke, and it sounded like thunder, it says the thunder itself uttered something. The word uttered in the Greek is the word "laleó," which means "to talk". (Biblehub.com) Another definition is to emit a sound. Therefore, the sound of God itself speaks, and man, when he carries it, is simply an instrument that produces the sound. This is why the bible says in 2 Corinthians 4:7 (KJV) that, *"we have this treasure in earthen vessels, that the excellency of the power may be of God, and not of us."* When sound flows through us, man will know that it's not natural, but this could've only come through a deity from another world. We, as believers, know that it's by the power of God.

A great question that man must then ask themselves is, "Are we speaking ourselves, or are we allowing the sound of God to flow through us"? God doesn't only send His agents with secrets; He sends them with sound. Matthew 24:31 (KJV) say, *"And he shall send his angels with a great sound of a trumpet, and they shall gather together his elect from the four winds, from one end of heaven to the other."* Notice God will send His angels with a sound to fulfill an assignment. In many other places in scripture, God sends His angels to individuals to reveal the secrets of God to them. Therefore, secrets go best with sound because God is just as interested in giving His people a distinct sound as He is in giving them a deep secret. Natural thunder is caused and produced by lightning. In scripture, when light is mentioned, it deals with revelation. Therefore, after one releases the mind of God, the sound of God should flow with it. According to almanac.com, the sound of thunder travels and can be heard about 15 miles from the nearest lightning bolt. This is what happened with Israel. Their sound could be heard far away.

John, the revelator, in speaking of the voice of Jesus while he was in the Spirit on the Lord's Day, identified it with two different sounds. The sound of a trumpet (Revelation 1:10) and the sound of many waters (Revelation 1:15). Jesus didn't just release words; He released sound.

Satan, formerly known as Lucifer, was the worship leader in heaven and understands the importance of sound. Therefore, Satan, in his endeavors for the kingdom of darkness, releases a sound as he goes about (1 Peter 5:8). If Satan and his agents understand the importance of releasing sound, then God's people should also know how important it is to release the sound of God. Psalms 104:7 (NIV), *"But at your rebuke the waters fled, at the sound of your thunder they took to flight."*

If God, when He spoke, released a sound of thunder and the waters moved and obeyed, then that is a sign to the believer that our sound commands and causes change to happen. Your sound causes your shift. The Prophet Elisha called for a minstrel who could release a sound into the atmosphere. Not just any sound but the sound of the Lord. How do we know that the sound that the minstrel released was of the Lord? Because when the sound came, the hand of the Lord came upon Elisha at that moment. In the Old Testament, musicians would be brought in to invite the presence of the Lord and to cast an evil presence out. However, these musicians in the Old Testament didn't just release any kind of sound, but a pure sound, and when they did, God responded to them. Satan and demons also responded to a pure sound.

The Counter To Sound: The Dumb Spirit

A dumb spirit is a spirit that causes one not to be able to speak. Jesus dealt with this spirit quite often in His ministry. When this spirit affects members of the body of Christ or a church, it causes people not to speak, and then the sound of the Lord does not flow out of them. The enemy would love nothing more than for a church to be silent. Silence could be a sign of defeat, although being loud doesn't necessarily mean victory. Nevertheless, the body of Christ must guard itself against this spirit because it shuts people down from speaking. After all, the enemy understands that when God's people release God's Word or the word of the Lord out of their mouth, his tactics are exposed. This spirit has an assignment to counter sound with silence.

Sound & Atmosphere

In Matthew 26:73, after Peter was approached by a servant girl in the courtyard of where he was, he denied knowing and being with Jesus, others came up to him and said, *"Surely thou also art one of them, for thy speech betrayeth thee."* The CSB translation says, *"You really are one of them, since even your accent gives you away."* An accent is cultivated based on where a person spends the majority of their time and with whom they spend most of their time. Peter couldn't deny knowing Jesus because his speech, sound, and accent gave him away. When a person spends time in prayer and being intimate with the Father, ascending into the heavens with God, they will eventually sound like God. They also carry the atmosphere of where they've been within them. A person carrying and releasing the sound of heaven will shift an entire atmosphere. A person carrying an atmosphere of heaven will also automatically release the sound of heaven because sound and atmosphere go hand in hand. It is important to know that your sound will determine your atmosphere, and your atmosphere will determine your sound. Mary wasn't just carrying a baby (Jesus); she was carrying an atmosphere (Jesus) within her. The atmosphere within her was so powerful that the atmosphere that was in Elizabeth (John the Baptist) responded to the atmosphere in Mary

(Jesus). Elizabeth's baby, John the Baptist, leaped according to Luke 1:41 (KJV), *"And it came to pass, that, when Elisabeth heard the salutation of Mary, the babe leaped in her womb; and Elisabeth was filled with the Holy Ghost."* It's very important to recognize that in Luke 1:41 that Elizabeth HEARD THE SALUTATION OF MARY, and the baby leaped. This means that Mary released a sound by saying something. When you carry a true atmosphere of heaven, the atmosphere within you will cause others around you to respond, saved or not, whether they want to or not. Her sound came because of what she carried, which was Jesus (an atmosphere), and because what she carried caused her to release a sound, it caused Elizabeth's life to change. She was filled with the Holy Spirit. Elizabeth was recorded in scripture as the first person in the New Testament who was filled with the Holy Spirit. Spiritually, Elizabeth advanced because she encountered someone with the right atmosphere. She benefited from Mary's atmosphere and walked in what wasn't released until the day of Pentecost many years later. She was ahead because when you encounter an atmosphere of heaven, you are encountering the mind and power of God.

    Those who carry an atmosphere of heaven have access to God's mind and have His power. This is why God wants His people with clean hands and a pure heart; what we carry is so powerful and vital to not only ourselves but also to those who we encounter and are assigned to our voice. Dr. Shaun Ferguson said years ago, "We can benefit from where the man of God has been." Meaning that the man of God has been to a place in the realm of the spirit and brought where he's been to those who he's encountering and to those assigned to his voice, and they can access that place as well.

Crossover

Nehemiah and the builders finished the wall in the month of Elul in 52 days. The word Elul is a word that comes from the Akkadian language in Babylon that the Jews became familiar with and adapted from their 70 years there. It means "harvest" and deals with bringing in crops and income. Elul is also a time of preparation for Jews for the entrance into the month of Tishrei, which is the first month in the Jewish calendar or the seventh month if it starts counting from the month Nisan in Babylon. Tishrei is the month of the High Holy Days, such as Rosh Hashanah and Yom Kippur. Rosh Hashanah and Yom Kippur represent the beginning of a time. Nehemiah and the builders finished the wall during a time of harvest. Despite great opposition and resistance, none of it could prevent the manifestation of the harvest that God had for His people in its ordained season and time. When it's your time to reap a harvest, you will reap it if you are in place to reap. It's important to keep going despite resistance because, at the appointed time, a harvest will come forth. What if when Sanballat, Tobiah, Geshem, and the rest of the co-conspirators that were in cohorts to stop Nehemiah had discouraged him and the builders from building? They would've crossed over into Elul, the time of harvest, and missed it because they abandoned their assignment and missed what God wanted to do through them. Sometimes one can be in the right season of their ordained harvest, and yet be in the wrong place. Therefore, they can't see or receive the harvest that God wants to release to them. Galations 5:9 (KJV) says, *"And let us not be weary in well doing: for in due season we shall reap, if we faint not."* Nehemiah and the Jews didn't become weary in their well-doing of building; then in due season, which was Elul, they reaped their harvest. Perhaps you are reading this, and you are functioning in your assignment and being faithful, but you've yet to see the manifestation of harvest. Rather, that's through a seed you've sown, a promise in the word of God, or a promise through a prophetic word. "Dear reader, know that your season will come, and you will complete what you've started by the grace of God because anything that God starts, He finishes."

The time in which Nehemiah and the builders also finished building the wall was significant because it was in Elul, which is the eve month before Tishrei. The transition of Elul into Tishrei represents a crossover. A crossover into something new and fresh. Nehemiah and the builders finishing the wall during this time was God telling Nehemiah something that we learn from. He was telling Nehemiah that He wasn't going to allow him to cross over into a new place (Elul) with an old assignment that was for his yesterday (everything before chapter Nehemiah 7). God wanted to complete what He had started in Nehemiah. In Genesis 32, when Jacob was crossing the Jabbok River, those that were with him crossed, but he couldn't crossover yet because God wanted to do a work in him. God wanted to change his name from Jacob to Israel before he crossed over. God didn't want Jacob crossing over into an assignment that was for Israel. It was at this point that Israel received responsibility for his assignment. The children of Israel couldn't cross over into the promised land with unbelief and doubt in their hearts. There is no such thing as a divine crossover with an old strategy and mentality. If we continue to function in the old, it will disrupt what God wants to do in the now. Crossovers are important. In scripture, Jesus either told His disciples, "let us go to the other side," or He Himself crossed to the other side (meaning another place by boat), especially after fulfilling a ministry assignment in a particular region. After He had fulfilled an assignment in a particular region, He understood the importance of going into new territories and not staying in the same place where He had already completed His assignment.

Nehemiah's assignment was so much more than building the wall. He had an apostolic and prophetic assignment to be a governor, bring order to the house of God, and expose what and who was illegitimate. He also had an assignment and charge to shift an economy and galvanize vessels into purpose. He couldn't spend all his time building the wall. There was more that God wanted him to do. He only had a limited amount of time before he was to return to the King. As Nehemiah was faithful to his assignment, he crossed over into Tishrei and even beyond that with a greater level of responsibility. Nehemiah's life is a prime example of the more faithful you are to the place that God has called you to or what He's called you to do, the more He will elevate you and give you more responsibility.

The Forging Of Something New

Matthew 9:16-17 (KJV) – "No man putteth a piece of new cloth unto an old garment, for that which is put in to fill it up taketh from the garment, and the rent is made worse. Neither do men put new wine into old bottles: else the bottles break, and the wine runneth out, and the bottles perish: but they put new wine into new bottles, and both are preserved."

God, in this hour, is forging a new skin. It is very important that man doesn't attempt to box the new that God is ushering in into the old. God doesn't and will not give a move of God to a people who are still functioning according to an old era or in an outdated system. So, as He forges something new, there are preludes that must and will precede this forging. Four of those will be discussed in this chapter.

1. Separation

Nehemiah 13:1-3 (KJV) – "On that day they read in the book of Moses in the audience of the people; and therein was found written, that the Ammonite and the Moabite should not come into the congregation of God for ever; Because they met not the children of Israel with bread and with water, but hired Balaam against them, that he should curse them: howbeit our God turned the curse into a blessing. Now it came to pass, when they had heard the law, that they separated from Israel all the mixed multitude."

The term "a mixed multitude" originates from when the children of Israel left Egypt. They had involved themselves with Egyptians in marriages and had children that were mixed in nationality, being both Israelite and Egyptian (Exodus 12:38).

A mixed multitude represents blending. Physical blending leads to spiritual blending, which is blending due to compromise and direct spiritual blending. Merriam-webster defines blend as a transitive verb that means to combine or associate so that the separate constituents or the line of demarcation cannot be distinguished. It is always the attempt of one who spiritually blends to cause it not to be able to be distinguished or detected by others. This is one of the reasons why discernment and sensitivity to the Holy Spirit are so imperative because without those two factors, one can be deceived. Nouns for the word "blend" are "mingle," "combine," "put together," "stir," "whisk," "fold in," "jumble," and "merge." Blending contaminates. Physical blending between individuals of the Kingdom of God and darkness is so dangerous because it is light and darkness blending. Eventually, because it is one of the Kingdom of

God compromised to connect with the one of the kingdom of darkness, the light of the one of the Kingdom of God will be put out.

Another outcome could be that the one of the Kingdom of God allows the physical blending to cause them to land and stay in a compromising place. The reason they will stay in a compromising place is because they see nothing wrong with the blend that they've allowed to happen. They'll think they have light, but it's darkness that has overshadowed all the light within them. The Apostle Paul, in teaching the church of Corinth in 2Corinthians 6:16-17 (KJV), said *"And what agreement hath the temple of God with idols? for ye are the temple of the living God; as God hath said, I will dwell in them, and walk in them; and I will be their God, and they shall be my people. Wherefore come out from among them, and be ye separate, saith the Lord, and touch not the unclean thing; and I will receive you."* He asked a very profound question, "what agreement hath the temple of God with idols?" Therefore, if something in a believer agrees with something of darkness, eventually, they'll compromise, which will drive the light out. This leads to spiritual blending, and this is where the church of the Lord Jesus is now. Blending has crept in and must be evicted as God forges something new. In this new and current culture, there is a blending of doctrines: The Holy Bible—biblical truth mixed with information from other religions' doctrines and worldly views. There has been a blending of sounds in music. Secular sounds, chords, and strings are mixed in with holy music to create a sound. This must be discerned and evicted. There has been a blending in worship of biblical and non-biblical words to create praise and worship songs. The culture and climate of blending must be dealt with at its core. Israel separated themselves from the mixed multitude after they were confronted with the word of God. They separated themselves from everyone that wasn't totally an Israelite. In life, as a believer, one of the greatest ways to maintain victory and integrity is to separate yourself from who and what is not like God. Our prayer to God should always be, "Lord, if my connection to them or this will cause me to be spiritually contaminated and shut down the anointing on my life, then I don't want to be connected to it. Show me every hindrance that I need to remove, then give me the grace and strength to remove it or them out of my life."

Prophet Vince Williams once told me, "You can't maintain your purity holding on to relationships that God never ordained." The word of God, along with apostolic and prophetic voices, will be what confronts and evicts blending.

2. Cleansing

Nehemiah 13:4-8 (KJV) – "*4 And before this, Eliashib the priest, having the oversight of the chamber of the house of our God, was allied unto Tobiah:5 And he had prepared for him a great chamber, where aforetime they laid the meat offerings, the frankincense, and the vessels, and the tithes of the corn, the new wine, and the oil, which was commanded to be given to the Levites, and the singers, and the porters; and the offerings of the priests.6 But in all this time was not I at Jerusalem: for in the two and thirtieth year of Artaxerxes king of Babylon came I unto the king, and after certain days obtained I leave of the king:7 And I came to Jerusalem, and understood of the evil that Eliashib did for Tobiah, in preparing him a chamber in the courts of the house of God.8 And it grieved me sore: therefore I cast forth all the household stuff to Tobiah out of the chamber.*"

What started in John 13, as Jesus was washing His Apostles to demonstrate the power and importance of serving another, turned into a time of great revelation being released from Jesus because of Peter. What Peter initially resisted, he afterward embraced. Peter initially forbade Jesus from washing his feet because he didn't understand at that moment what Jesus was doing. Jesus responded to Peter's forbidding by telling him, "*If I wash thee not, thou hast no part with me.*" The Lord will never be a part of what He can't clean or what is not pure. This is the reason that Nehemiah commanded that the chambers in the house of God that Tobiah was once occupying be cleansed. Nehemiah didn't suggest; he commanded, which means it was mandatory because God will never put new into old. After Peter received greater revelation from Jesus, he responded to Jesus by telling Him in John 13:9 (KJV), *"Lord, not only my feet but my hands and my head."* Peter was asking what would cause him to ascend. Psalms 24:3 teaches who will ascend in the hill of the Lord and into His place: he that hath clean hands and a pure heart. When Peter asked Jesus to wash his hands, he was asking to do something that would cause him to ascend to supernatural places in God by the Spirit of God. Interestingly, Peter also asked to wash his head. To understand this better, you must understand what's connected to the head and how important it is to keep those gates clean because those are some of the ways that the Lord communicates with man.

Gates connected to the head are:

<u>Mind</u>: This is a gate that receives information. This contributes to a man's mindset, whether managed correctly or not, it determines one's identity.

The Apostle Paul, in writing to the church at Rome said in Romans 12:2 (KJV), said *"And be not conformed to this world: but be ye transformed by the renewing of your mind, that ye may prove what is that good, and acceptable, and perfect, will of God."* Allowing the wrong information into this gate prohibits you from being transformed by the renewing of your mind. Proverbs 23:7 (KJV*)* says*, For as he thinketh in his heart, so is he…"*

Eyes: This gate receives information that affects a man's desire, feeds his soul, and affects his belief systems.

Psalms 119:37 (ESV) says*, "Turn my eyes from looking at worthless things; and give me life in your ways."* David was being intentional in covering his eye gate by asking God to help him to stop looking at worthless things. Worthless things don't bring edification to man's spirit or contribute to his spiritual growth and development. They also don't bring glory to God. A high percentage of worthless things enter the eye via television, the internet, and social media. What you allow into your physical eye gate affects your spiritual eyes and your vision into the spirit realm. I've discovered in my walk with the Lord as a seer that whenever I have allowed carnality into my eye gate long enough, it has affected my ability to see and discern. It impacted what God wanted me to see and on the level that I normally saw because carnality and purity can't coexist and function together in the same space. David's motive and the reason behind him writing Psalms 119:37 was about his desire to change and for God to give him an appetite for the things of God. The Apostle Paul, in writing to the church at Corinth in 2 Corinthians 5:7 (KJV), said, *"For we walk by faith and not sight."* If a man sees something long enough, it will affect his faith. Therefore, mature believers will separate themselves from the sight of what will affect their faith.

Ears: This gate receives information that establishes concepts and perspectives and most importantly a man's belief system.

The Apostle Paul, in writing to the church at Rome, said in Romans 10:17 (KJV), *"So then faith cometh by hearing, and hearing by the word of God."* If faith comes by hearing, then so does fear and foolishness. What man allows into their ears determines what they have faith in. Again, in my walk with the Lord, whenever I've allowed the wrong words, sounds, and information into my ear gate long enough, it has affected my ability to hear. My frequency to be off from God and Heaven. In Genesis 35, God told Jacob to go to Bethel, and one of the instructions Jacob gave his family was to get rid of their foreign gods.

Genesis 35:4, the Bible says that Jacob's family gave him their earrings. They confronted what was in their ears and what they were letting in their ears. This is symbolic and indicative of a reality that man must be intentional about covering their ear gate and be careful about what they allow into it.

<u>Mouth</u>: This gate is imperative for effective communication and creativity.

Proverbs 18:21 (KJV) says, *"Death and life are in the power of the tongue: and they that love it shall eat the fruit thereof."* Therefore, a man confessing what's contrary to what God said about him will be detrimental to his life and everything around him. Jesus said in John 6:63 (KJV) *"The words that I speak to you are spirit, and they are life."* Words are spirit and create either life or death. As man releases words out of his mouth naturally, those words will cause conception and birthing in the spirit realm, and eventually, manifestation transpires. What Jesus said in Mark 11:23 gives insight and clarity that man will have whatsoever he says, whether good or bad. Wrong communication can be destructive to a man. This is one of the reasons why the scripture warns against lying, gossiping, and all corrupt communication.

Psalms 101:7 (KJV) – "He that worketh deceit shall not dwell within my house: he that telleth lies shall not tarry in my sight."

Proverbs 20:19 (NASB) – "One who goes about as a slanderer reveals secrets; Therefore do not associate with a gossip."

Proverbs 11:9 (MSG) – "The loose tongue of the godless spreads destruction; the common sense of the godly preserves them."

Ephesians 4:29 (KJV) – "Let no corrupt communication proceed out of your mouth, but that which is good to the use of edifying, that it may minister grace unto the hearers."

Proverbs 29:11 (KJV) – "A fool uttereth all his mind: but a wise man keepeth it in till afterwards."

When the Lord came down to meet the children of Israel on Mount Sinai in Exodus 19, Moses first gave them some prerequisites as the prelude to this happening. One of those prerequisites in Exodus 19:10 was for the children of Israel to wash their clothes. In the Old Testament, the law required the children of Israel to wash their clothes on many occasions. The children of Israel washing represented them not having anything unclean touching them. When people are analyzing their lives, they should not only look at what they are touching but who or what is touching them. Believers should be careful of what and who gets close to them because of the anointing on their lives. One must guard the anointing on their life with everything they have. One guards the anointing on their life by not allowing anything unclean near them or to touch them because of what they carry. To allow that which is unclean around you is to allow uncleanliness around your anointing. This can affect the anointing from operating in your life because of what has been allowed to near it. Before the priest could wear the holy garments in the Old Testament, their body would have to be clean. The washing of the body is an outward expression of an inward reality of cleansing. When Jesus called Bartimaeus, who was blind, in Mark 10:49 to come to Him, Bartimaeus first abandoned his garments and then came. Blind Bartimaeus's garments contributed to his identity. Once he removed what was touching him, which also solidified his identity as a beggar, then his identity changed.

Nehemiah begins the cleansing of the house of God by casting out what the high priest Elishab allowed Tobiah to bring in it. Much worldliness is blatantly on display in the house of God, and it has not been confronted. However, the Lord is summoning His apostles to cast out of the house of God what has been brought in, and to speak judgment concerning these things. There is an evil that has been done by allowing a worldly spirit into the house of God and to sit and rest in the house of God confrontation-free in the name of relationships. The Bible says that Eliashib, the high priest, was allied unto Tobiah, which means he didn't confront what was ushered into the house of God because of who was ushering it. However, there is a remnant of believers that will rebuke no matter who or what it is. Nehemiahs are arising as apostolic voices and will bring correction to areas in the church and body of Christ that are out of order. Purification will follow this correction, and as a result, a reverential respect for the house of the Lord. Tobiah was in the house of God taking up space, but his presence was insignificant. Tobiah was taking up room but had no relationship. The space and room Tobiah was occupying demanded that one have a relationship with God. As God brings cleansings to His house and people, He will remove those off the scene who are illegally occupying space and offices and are hazards in the house of God and to the body of Christ. God will never change His mind about the church that He wants to present unto Himself. A glorious church, not having spot or wrinkle, but holy and without blemish according to Ephesians 5:27.

3. Order - God will bring order where there has been disorder.

Nehemiah 13:9 (KJV) – "Then I commanded, and they cleansed the chambers: and thither brought I again the vessels of the house of God, with the meat offering and the frankincense."

1 Corinthians 14:40 (KJV) says, *"Let all things be done decently and in order."* This scripture was given to the church at Corinth to seal directions as to how God wanted His church to operate in corporate worship. It included when speaking in tongues, manifestations of the Holy Spirit, and other directives. This is God's heart for His church collectively in every area. God loves order and can't move where there's disorder; this is the reason why correction is coming. The word order in Greek is the word "taxis," and one of the ways that this word is used is as a "regular arrangement." This means that the order that God is bringing back to the house of God is the order that He originally intended to operate in. God ushers in newness as He moves (Isaiah 49:17), but He's the same yesterday, today, and forevermore (Hebrews 13:8). God did a new thing for His people by sending Jesus Christ into the earth. The whole purpose of bringing Christ was to get man to the place where Adam was in the garden before he sinned. This was His

original intent for man. Nehemiah brought the vessels of God back to the Lord's house. This means that there was once a time that the vessels were once there. He simply instituted and ushered back into place what was never supposed to leave. There was a revisiting of what was foundational, that never should've left to begin with.

4. Alert

Nehemiah 13:10 - 11 (KJV) – "[10] And I perceived that the portions of the Levites had not been given them: for the Levites and the singers, that did the work, were fled every one to his field.[11] Then contended I with the rulers, and said, Why is the house of God forsaken? And I gathered them together, and set them in their place."

God is alerting those who have or perhaps have thought that they aren't valuable and necessary to what God is doing in this era. The Levites were necessary and important to what God was doing during Nehemiah's time; though they didn't see much harvest or reward, they remained faithful. The Levites could've been discouraged and deemed their labor as ineffective. God had to alert them through Nehemiah that their harvest and reward were coming. The Levites went back to their own fields after they finished serving in the house of God, which means they were content with their serving. The Levites served God's people from their hearts. It wasn't about a dollar; it was about deliverance for the people. The hearts of the Levites were pure, which made them valuable to God for what needed to be done. Those who have been overlooked but have kept serving with integrity are getting ready to be rewarded. This is a prophetic promise with apostolic assurance. This also meant that their gifts were pure because they didn't have a price tag on themselves. The Lord will confront this capitalistic culture where money is prioritized over ministry. The Levites represent a generation who did not and will not put a price on the grace and anointing. If your love for God exceeds your inspiration for ministry, then your motives are pure. Apostolic voices are getting ready with their voice to declare a greater level of purpose by the Spirit of God to those who have been overlooked.

At the time Nehemiah began his confronting, what the people were releasing from and out of them didn't match the dispensation and era they were in. Nehemiah had to confront this as a man of God because there had to be a forging. The people had to be challenged and provoked for change to occur.

God is going to release three things to His people that they'll release in this new dispensation as this forging takes place.

Nehemiah 13:12-13 (KJV) – "^{12} *Then brought all Judah the tithe of the corn and the new wine and the oil unto the treasuries.* ^{13} *And I made treasurers over the treasuries, Shelemiah the priest, and Zadok the scribe, and of the Levites, Pedaiah: and next to them was Hanan the son of Zaccur, the son of Mattaniah: for they were counted faithful, and their office was to distribute unto their brethren."*

Corn will be released. Corn in the natural is food, but in the Spirit, it is symbolic of the word of God and the mind and heart of God through revelation. Deuteronomy 25:4 (KJV) *says "Thou shalt not muzzle the ox when he treadeth out the corn."* There is coming a release of new revelations, new downloads, and insight from the Lord.

New wine will be released. Wine is a type of the Spirit. However, this wasn't just wine; it was new wine, indicating the Spirit of God doing something fresh. There is coming a release of new revelation, new downloads, and insight from the Lord. Ephesians 5:18 says, *"And be not drunk with wine, wherein is excess; but be filled with the Spirit."* Therefore, wine is a type of Spirit. We are coming into an era and time where the Lord will begin to pour out His Spirit upon all flesh. There will be great moves of the Spirit that will be birthed across the world. This move will bring deliverance, miracles, signs, and wonders.

Oil will be released. Oil is symbolic of God's presence, anointing, and power. In the Old Testament, the oil would be poured on an individual as a sign of the presence of God and for that individual to accomplish the work they had been anointed to do. The greatness of the presence of the Lord will be released and revealed in those who are working in the Kingdom. The Lord will begin to place His anointing on those who are clean vessels. The anointing will be felt and manifested like never before in public corporate gatherings amongst the Body of Christ. We will see believers operate in power as it was in the days of the church of Acts because of the oil that is being released.

The people already had corn, wine, and oil. They just weren't releasing it in the dispensation they were supposed to be releasing it in. It took Nehemiah, an apostolic voice, to challenge and provoke the people of Judah. As long as the people of Judah weren't releasing their tithes, the house of God was forsaken, and the Levites weren't getting what was due to them, causing them to need a breakthrough. This story is a template of what the Lord will do as He forges something new by alerting those who need to know they are important to what God wants to do in the earth. When those who have a grace, an anointing, and/or mantle on their lives to bless others don't release what's been released to them it causes others to be delayed and hindered. As you read this, I need you to understand that someone needs the revelation that you carry. Someone needs the Spirit of God, and the atmosphere inside you to be released. Someone needs the anointing that you carry, and we can't hold it back because the anointing on our lives is not for us, it's for others. According to Isaiah 10:27 (KJV), *"And it shall come to pass in that day, that his burden shall be taken away from off thy shoulder, and his yoke from off thy neck, and the yoke shall be destroyed because of the anointing."* There are people in bondage that need the anointing, and we've been assigned to release it. Your disobedience will cause others to be frustrated. The corn, wine, and oil will be released in the house of God, causing great explosions of glory, which will be seen in revival.

Nehemiah confronted the leaders and rulers of the house of God that had overlooked the Levites, who were supposed to be rewarded, but it had never been given to them. The people stopped tithing prior to Nehemiah returning to Jerusalem the second time. During the time of Nehemiah's absence, other voices for God perhaps could have dealt with this but didn't. This seasoned apostle with jurisdiction in the spiritual and physical realm dealt with issues that needed a mature voice to confront and correct. Nehemiah, however, didn't start there, but as time progressed, he matured and became a seasoned voice in and to his generation. God's ultimate desire is that emerging Nehemiahs eventually become seasoned and mature voices that have jurisdiction to deal with controversy and topics that require maturity in the body of Christ to deal with. Nehemiah started off as an emerging voice at the beginning of the book of Nehemiah, but by the end, he was a seasoned voice. This shows that God is interested in the longevity of those whom He has called. So many people get stuck on and at their emergence, or peak, but once there's a leveling off in ministry, they become ordinary and never reach the apex of what God wanted them to be. If we follow the Holy Spirit, He will guide us in all truth and won't allow us to get stuck in anything. He will help us to reach the level that the Father desires us to reach.

Nehemiah did much confronting in Nehemiah 13. However, he didn't just confront a country but cultures. Emerging Nehemiahs are called to confront cultures. End-time cultures are cultures within the church of the Lord Jesus Christ that will hinder what God wants to do. There are cultures within the world that are displeasing to God, and cultures within systems that don't uphold the standard of God. Apostle Dannie Williams, during a message that he taught called "A Prophetic Response to the Present Culture," addressed 5 cultures that need to be prepared for in the last days.

Culture Of Carnality

1 Timothy 3:1-5 (KJV) – "[1] This know also, that in the last days perilous times shall come. [2] For men shall be lovers of their own selves, covetous, boasters, proud, blasphemers, disobedient to parents, unthankful, unholy, [3] Without natural affection, trucebreakers, false accusers, incontinent, fierce, despisers of those that are good, [4] Traitors, heady, highminded, lovers of pleasures more than lovers of God; [5] Having a form of godliness, but denying the power thereof: from such turn away.

Culture Of Collapse

2 Thessalonians 2:1-3 (KJV) Now we beseech you, brethren, by the coming of our Lord Jesus Christ, and by our gathering together unto him, 2 That ye be not soon shaken in mind, or be troubled, neither by spirit, nor by word, nor by letter as from us, as that the day of Christ is at hand. 3 Let no man deceive you by any means: for that day shall not

come, except there come a falling away first, and that man of sin be revealed, the son of perdition.

Culture Of Chaos

Matthew 24:3-13 (KJV) – "³ And as he sat upon the mount of Olives, the disciples came unto him privately, saying, Tell us, when shall these things be? and what shall be the sign of thy coming, and of the end of the world? ⁴ And Jesus answered and said unto them, Take heed that no man deceive you. ⁵ For many shall come in my name, saying, I am Christ; and shall deceive many. ⁶ And ye shall hear of wars and rumours of wars: see that ye be not troubled: for all these things must come to pass, but the end is not yet. ⁷ For nation shall rise against nation, and kingdom against kingdom: and there shall be famines, and pestilences, and earthquakes, in divers places. ⁸ All these are the beginning of sorrows. ⁹ Then shall they deliver you up to be afflicted, and shall kill you: and ye shall be hated of all nations for my name's sake. ¹⁰ And then shall many be offended, and shall betray one another, and shall hate one another. ¹¹ And many false prophets shall rise, and shall deceive many. ¹² And because iniquity shall abound, the love of many shall wax cold. ¹³ But he that shall endure unto the end, the same shall be saved."

Culture Of Counterfeits

Matthew 24:23-26 (KJV) – "²³ Then if any man shall say unto you, Lo, here is Christ, or there; believe it not. ²⁴ For there shall arise false Christs, and false prophets, and shall shew great signs and wonders; insomuch that, if it were possible, they shall deceive the very elect. ²⁵ Behold, I have told you before. ²⁶ Wherefore if they shall say unto you, Behold, he is in the desert; go not forth: behold, he is in the secret chambers; believe it not."

Culture Of Compromise

Matthew 24:36-39 (KJV) – "³⁶ But of that day and hour knoweth no man, no, not the angels of heaven, but my Father only. ³⁷ But as the days of Noah were, so shall also the coming of the Son of man be. ³⁸ For as in the days that were before the flood they were eating and drinking, marrying and giving in marriage, until the day that Noe entered into the ark, ³⁹ And knew not until the flood came, and took them all away; so shall also the coming of the Son of man be."

A New Era: Revival

Jerusalem was in a totally better state in Nehemiah chapter 7 than it was in Nehemiah 2:17, as the bible says in Nehemiah 2:17 (NIV) that *"Jerusalem lies in ruins, and its gate have been burned with fire."* Then in Nehemiah 7:4, Nehemiah refers to Jerusalem as "great." So there had to have been progress if he went from calling the city a place of ruins to a great city. It wasn't the same Jerusalem after God used Nehemiah to build it up again. When Nehemiahs are emerging, it represents a new time and era. In Nehemiah chapter 7, Nehemiah noticed that Jerusalem wasn't populated like it once was, at which point God gave him a strategy on repopulating Jerusalem. The Church of Jesus Christ is not the same church that it was before the 2020 pandemic that it will be after the shutdowns and quarantine. Nehemiah understands what every pastor in the world faced during the 2020 pandemic when they had a church full of empty pews and everything following it. Catastrophic events transpired in the land of Judah and Jerusalem, and when Nehemiah came into the land, he was tasked with repopulating it. In a time where church attendance has drastically declined because of a plague called COVID-19, people want to know, where does the church and leaders go from here? The church can't go back to where it once was, it must now exceed it. The world will not be the same again after the year 2020.

Revival is the answer! Revival is happening! Apostle Dannie Williams said in 2022 that, "It's one thing for us (the church) to gather for glory, but it's another thing for glory to gather us (the church)." Glory will gather the church together again, and the church will experience a harvest of souls. Glory will be a great attraction; however, it will not be the main one. The cross and the Christ of the cross will always be the main attraction. The strategy that God gave Nehemiah was to gather the nobles, the rulers, and the people so that they might be reckoned by genealogy. After Nehemiah did this, he then knew who was in the land with him. After that order came, God took care of the rest. The people were positioned for revival. Be thankful for who's with you. God took who was in the land already with Nehemiah to do His will. The Lord will use who's currently standing with leaders to do what He wants to do and add at the same time. Nehemiah 7:73 (KJV) says, *"So the priests, and the Levites, and the porters, and the singers, and some of the people, and the Nethinims, and all Israel, dwelt in their cities; and when the seventh month came, the children of Israel were in their cities."* When the seventh month came, the children were in their cities, which means that there was order. It set the stage for what God was going to do because God can't move in disorder. The seventh month in the Jewish calendar is Tishri. Tishri is a month of new beginnings in the Jewish calendar. This means that the children of Israel had entered a new place and time. The world has entered a new era, and in this new era and time revival is happening.

After Nehemiah chapter 7, revival had hit the land. After chapter 6, you see the book of Nehemiah shift from building the framework for which the move of God is housed to the spiritual aspects of ministry. God sent revival to a people that had stepped into a new realm in him. This is where the church and world are currently in 2023. We've stepped into a new place, era, and time, and God is sending revival amid dark times. The days may be dark, but the light is very bright. Specifically, revival has hit America. A move of God is happening. This move of God will not have anyone's name on it. Ezra was the one that God used in scripture to bring pure worship back to the temple; however, this new move of God will not have any person's name on it. Peter, on the day of Pentecost, stood up and began to preach, but what was happening had nothing to do with Peter. He was simply the vessel God was using. Nehemiah chapters 8-12 are a template of what the Holy Spirit is doing in America. Understand that I am in no way writing about a recipe for seeing revival because there is no recipe to see revival. The manifestation of revival is at and by God's sovereignty.

Nehemiah 8:1 (KJV) – "And all the people gathered themselves together as one man into the street that was before the water gate; and they spake unto Ezra the scribe to bring the book of the law of Moses, which the Lord had commanded to Israel."

(And all the people gathered themselves together as one man into the street that was before the water gate;)

All the people came together as one. This is significant of the reality that revival is happening in the church of the Lord Jesus Christ as a whole and not among a certain denomination, nationality of people, or people of certain status.

It's very important that emphasis be put on where the children of Israel gathered. They strategically gathered at the water gate to hear what God would say to them. Water is a type of the Spirit. Nobody instructed them where to gather; they were just sensitive enough to know which gate to gather at. As revival is happening, people will no longer gather at any and every house of worship. People will know when and where wells have dried up and there is no life. People will gather where the Spirit of God is moving, and His power is on display.

(and they spake unto Ezra the scribe to bring the book of the law of Moses, which the Lord had commanded to Israel.)

The children of Israel put a demand on the anointing of Ezra's life to release the word of God because of their hunger for God. There are people who are hungry and thirsty for God and want to see His power demonstrated and manifested in the earth. As revival happens, the Lord is filling His people with more of Him and causing them to see His power manifested in the earth.

Matthew 5:6 (KJV) – "Blessed are they which do hunger and thirst after righteousness: for they shall be filled."

Matthew 5:8 (KJV) – "Blessed are the pure in heart: for they shall see God."

The children of Israel gathering in one place by the water gate is symbolic of people gathering where God is, with a desire to see Him move. An Acts chapter 2 encounter that will manifest and be at the forefront of this revival.

Acts 2:1-4 (KJV)– "¹ And when the day of Pentecost was fully come, they were all with one accord in one place. ² And suddenly there came a sound from heaven as of a rushing mighty wind, and it filled all the house where they were sitting.³ And there appeared unto them cloven tongues like as of fire, and it sat upon each of them.⁴ And they were all filled with the Holy Ghost, and began to speak with other tongues, as the Spirit gave them utterance."

Nehemiah 8:3 (KJV) – "And he read therein before the street that was before the water gate from the morning until midday, before the men and the women, and those that could understand; and the ears of all the people were attentive unto the book of the law."

(And he read therein before the street that was before the water gate from the morning until midday.)

The children were not in a rush but lingered in the presence of God. As revival happens, people will not rush to get out of the church or grieve the Spirit of God by putting Him on a time clock while He's moving. A clock has been one of the greatest hindrances to the continuation of the Spirit of God moving.

In Exodus 40:36-37 (KJV), the bible says, *"And when the cloud was taken up from over the tabernacle, the children of Israel went onward in all their journeys: 37 But if the cloud were not taken up, then they journeyed not till the day that it was taken up."*

The children of Israel, in the book of Exodus, didn't move while the cloud (the glory of the Lord) was in their midst. The cloud was the children of Israel's protection, and they knew they couldn't survive without it. When you rush from under or move away from a cloud, you move away from everything in the cloud. Miracles, signs, wonders, healing, deliverance, freedom, protection, provision, prophetic insight, the manifested presence and power of God, and everything man needs. Therefore, one's inability to sit with God and under a cloud costs more than one thinks. When one rushes from under a cloud, they distance themselves from what God has provided for them. Exodus 40:36-37 is a prophetic picture of a remnant that is arising and emerging. They are hungry and desperate for the glory of the Lord. Therefore, they will not watch the clock in church, hoping that they are out of the church by a certain time. They will allow God to do what He wants to do no matter how long it takes. They will linger in moments to get all that the Father wants to release in that moment. They will not disrespect what will deliver them. As revival happens in this era, the glory of God will be so respected and honored, and God will be able to do what He wants with no restrictions.

(and the ears of all the people were attentive unto the book of the law).

The children of Israel gave their attention to the word of God. Giving attention to the word of God and putting it first with no distractions give it permission to produce in one's life.

Nehemiah 8:4 (KJV) – "And Ezra the scribe stood upon a pulpit of wood, which they had made for the purpose; and beside him stood Mattithiah, and Shema, and Anaiah, and Urijah, and Hilkiah, and Maaseiah, on his right hand; and on his left hand, Pedaiah, and Mishael, and Malchiah, and Hashum, and Hashbadana, Zechariah, and Meshullam."

As revival is happening in America, the Lord is now giving true and pure vessels a platform to stand on before people. Those who have been in hiding will now emerge and be given a platform before people in a time of revival.

Nehemiah 8:9 (KJV) – "And Nehemiah, which is the Tirshatha, and Ezra the priest the scribe, and the Levites that taught the people, said unto all the people, This day is holy unto the Lord your God; mourn not, nor weep. For all the people wept, when they heard the words of the law."

The Apostle Paul, in writing to the church of Corinth in 2 Corinthians 7:10 (NLT) about their repentance, said, *"For the kind of sorrow God wants us to experience leads us away from sin and results in salvation. There's no regret for that kind of sorrow. But worldly sorrow, which lacks repentance, results in spiritual death."* The sorrow that the church of Corinth experienced is the same kind of sorrow that the children of Israel experienced. The sorrow that leads people away from sin and provokes them to draw nigh unto God.

(mourn not, nor weep. For all the people wept, when they heard the words of the law.)

As revival happens in America, people will respond to the word of God. The hearts of people will be open to the gospel of Jesus Christ as the Spirit of God does a work in the hearts of men.

Nehemiah 8:10 – "Then he said unto them, Go your way, eat the fat, and drink the sweet, and send portions unto them for whom nothing is prepared: for this day is holy unto our Lord: neither be ye sorry; for the joy of the Lord is your strength.)."

(Then he said unto them, Go your way, eat the fat, and drink the sweet, and send portions unto them for whom nothing is prepared:)

Nehemiah, as a prophet, told the people to celebrate what God was doing in their lives and in the land. He was telling them to not only focus on the fact that they had been convicted of their sins and felt broken. As God's voice in the earth, Nehemiah wanted them to focus on the fact that God had a plan to restore His people and show forth His greatness in their lives.

(for this day is holy unto our Lord: neither be ye sorry; for the joy of the Lord is your strength.)

The prophet was telling the people not to stay in a place of brokenness, but to understand that the joy of the Lord is their strength and would keep them moving forward. The Apostle Paul said in Romans 8:1 (KJV), *"There is therefore now no condemnation to them which are in Christ Jesus, who walk not after the flesh, but after the Spirit."* Some people become stuck in what they've done, and they don't think that God will ever forgive them. Yet God wants to restore joy and help His people understand that He's more concerned about their future than He is about their past. If a person wants to stay stuck in sorrow, it blocks the joy from coming in. In this great revival happening in America, people will experience the love of God and the forgiveness of God through grace. People will move from places of brokenness over past sins to a place of joy because of forgiveness and the plan that God has for them.

Nehemiah 8:15-16 (KJV) – "And that they should publish and proclaim in all their cities, and in Jerusalem, saying, Go forth unto the mount, and fetch olive branches, and pine branches, and myrtle branches, and palm branches, and branches of thick trees, to make booths, as it is written. So the people went forth, and brought them, and made themselves booths, every one upon the roof of his house, and in their courts, and in the courts of the house of God, and in the street of the water gate, and in the street of the gate of Ephraim."

The different branches and tree referred to in Nehemiah 8:15 are types and symbols. Men are types of trees and branches also referenced in Mark 8:24, Psalms 1:3 & John 15:5. The leaders of cities were told to go forth unto the mount. The mount that is being referred to is the Mount of Olives, but it is not limited to just that place. The leaders were told to go to a place where olives were. Olives produce oil after they've been squeezed. However, they were not told to go to a place of oil, but of olives. This place was on a mountain. A mountain is a high place in God, where revelation and instruction are released in scripture. This is where the Lord is looking for those who He wants to revive. God asked in Isaiah 6:8, "...*Whom shall I send, and who will go for us?*" The Prophet Isaiah responded to the Lord by saying, *"Here am I; send me."* This is significant of the reality of God specifically looking for those who are and have been in the mountains, who are ready to be stretched to see olives produce oil.

Jesus says in John 15:5 (KJV), *"I am the vine, ye are the branches: He that abideth in me, and I in him, the same bringeth forth much fruit: for without me ye can do nothing."* The word "branch" in Hebrew is the word "aleh," which comes from the word "alah," meaning "to go up," "ascend, or climb". (Biblehub.com) God is saying, "As revival is happening in the church of the Lord Jesus Christ, I'm looking for and using oil carriers who have ascended in me."

Pine branches in the original Hebrew are translated as oil trees. Oil trees in Hebrew is the word "shemen," which comes from the word "shamen," meaning "to grow fat." (Biblehub.com) It is also the word "fertile." In this, God is saying those whom He is using in revival will carry a heavy anointing. "Fat" is another word for "anointing" in the Old Testament. Those whom the hand of the Lord is upon will walk heavily in the anointing. They will be fertile, and fertile ground. They will be proven to be good ground for others to sow into because of their consistency, character, and compassion for others.

"Myrtle" in Hebrew is the word "hadas," which is the same as the word "hadom," and it means a stool, or footstool. (Biblehub.com) A stool or footstool is where you rest something. In this, God is saying, "I'm using those who have rested in my presence and have ascended in me."

"Palm" in Hebrew is the word "tamar," which is the same as the word "tomer," and it means "palm tree" or "post." (Biblehub.com) Palm trees represent flourishing, uprightness, and victory. In this, God is saying, "I'm using upright people who have been planted in the house of God and, as a result, are flourishing." He is using people who understand their rights and privileges as believers in Christ Jesus to see victory. Palm branches are those who live in the supernatural, move in the supernatural, and have their being in the supernatural because of God (Acts 17:28). These are supernatural agents who have ascended. During this time of revival, the purpose of them gathering olive, pine, myrtle, and branches of thick trees was to make booths. In the Old Testament, when it refers to booths, they are referring to a place of shelter. They were erected and used at the feast of Tabernacles. The children of Israel would gather branches and articles to create booths. They used specific branches and articles to construct the framework for what they were building. Not only did they use them, but they were intricate parts of what they were building. The types of people named above are intricate parts of God doing what He wants to do in revival. These anointed vessels together represent a great and powerful remnant that God is gathering.

(every one upon the roof of his house)

(Prophecy)

The olive, pine, myrtle, and branches of thick trees that were gathered to create booths were placed on each man on the roof of his house. A roof is a covering. God is intentional, especially with men who are present leaders in homes, now using them to shift the atmosphere of their homes. In the days to come, personal homes will experience revival separate from what God will do in the local church. Healings, miracles, deliverances, and breakthroughs will manifest in homes because those covering their families will arise in this era.

(and in their courts)

(Prophecy)

The olive, pine, myrtle, and branches of thick trees that were gathered to create booths were placed in their courts. The Lord is now causing these individuals to be placed in the courts of their assignments. As a result of their connection to people, people's lives will be changed.

(and in the courts of the house of God)

(Prophecy)

The olive, pine, myrtle, and branches of thick trees that were gathered to create booths were placed in the courts of the house of God.

This remnant of branches is being planted in the house of God to lead God's people into greater dimensions of who God is. Who they are will draw many to them. The house of God in this era and in the last days will be filled with people who will be supernatural, and they will raise up others to be supernatural. Also, as stated in the House of God in the 5-Fold Gift, there is a remnant that will cover God's people. Having a leader to cover your soul has always been important but will be critical in the last days.

(and in the street of the water gate)

(Prophecy)

The olive, pine, myrtle, and branches of thick trees that were gathered to create booths were placed in the street of the water gate. God will use these individuals as mighty evangelists as revival happens. Unusual and unexplainable manifestations of the Holy Spirit will occur as God uses them.

(and in the street of the gate of Ephraim)

(Prophecy)

The olive, pine, myrtle, and branches of thick trees that were gathered to create booths were placed in the street of the gate of Ephraim. Ephraim, as stated in the Walls, Gates, and Doors chapter, means double fruitfulness and increase. This remnant that is arising will live lives of double fruitfulness. Increase will be their portion because of where the Lord is positioning them. The favor of God will be on their lives, and as a result, they will never want for anything but will always have more than enough.

Nehemiah chapter 9 is a continuation of the revival that had hit the land from the previous chapter.

Nehemiah 9:1-2 (KJV) – "Now in the twenty and fourth day of this month the children of Israel were assembled with fasting, and with sack clothes, and earth upon them. 2 And the seed of Israel separated themselves from all strangers, and stood and confessed their sins, and the iniquities of their fathers."

A key point here is that the seed of Israel separated themselves from strangers. They knew that if they wanted to continue to flow in what God was doing in the land, it demanded separation. Repentance followed their separation from what was because repentance is an action. Revival isn't authentic if it doesn't drive the people experiencing it into a place of true repentance. This is because the more of God that man sees, the more man realizes how much he needs God.

Nehemiah 9:3 (KJV) – "And they stood up in their place, and read in the book of the law of the Lord their God one fourth part of the day; and another fourth part they confessed, and worshiped the Lord their God."

According to Nehemiah 9:3, these people spent a quarter of their days reading the word of God and another quarter of their days confessing their sins with their faces towards God or in worship to God. That's 50 percent of their day, which is half a day every day that they set aside for God and the things of God. These people had lives, jobs, and responsibilities. We know from reading the book of Nehemiah that these people were builders, guards, and people with governmental positions, amongst other things. Though they were people with lives, when God called for a time unto Himself, the people responded. This kills the argument of people who claim not to have time for the things of God because of all that they have going on in their lives. Understand that God doesn't send revival based on man's schedule. We must adjust our schedule to get on board with what God is doing. It will sometimes be an inconvenience to man, but those hungry don't care what they must do to get God. The hungry remnant is arising. There is a remnant that is just waiting for God to send revival.

Checking The Records

In this chapter the spirit of illegitimacy will be exposed so that it may be evicted. As the world has shifted into a new era it is important that this spirit is exposed and judged.

Nehemiah 7:5-6 (KJV) – "And my God put into mine heart to gather together the nobles, and the rulers, and the people, that they might be reckoned by genealogy. And I found a register of the genealogy of them which came up at the first, and found written therein,"

Nehemiah 7:61-64 (KJV) – "[61] And these were they which went up also from Telmelah, Telharesha, Cherub, Addon, and Immer: but they could not shew their father's house, nor their seed, whether they were of Israel.[62] The children of Delaiah, the children of Tobiah, the children of Nekoda, six hundred forty and two.[63] And of the priests: the children of Habaiah, the children of Koz, the children of Barzillai, which took one of the daughters of Barzillai the Gileadite to wife, and was called after their name.[64] These sought their register among those that were reckoned by genealogy, but it was not found: therefore were they, as polluted, put from the priesthood."

There is a spirit of illegitimacy that has crept into the church of the Lord Jesus Christ and is hiding behind a religious front and face. This spirit and the people who carry it have blended in with the real. Therefore, making it nearly impossible to spot them or locate the spirit, if not for revelation that comes through the gifts of the Spirit by the Holy Spirit and discernment. Dictionary.com defines "illegitimate" as unlawful and illegal. Also not sanctioned by law or custom. Those from Telmelah, which were Telharesha, Cherub, Addon, and Immer, were exposed because of what God put in Nehemiah's heart. Telmelah means "mound of salt" and was a place in Babylon. Salt is a flavor and gives taste to whatever goes in it. These were people whose aura rubbed off on others. God was intentional in why He told Nehemiah to check the records. This exposure is necessary because if this spirit and its assignment are not exposed, then there will be an intertwining between what's of the world and what's of God. Then, after a while, it won't be noticeable because the longer a thing lingers, the more acceptable it becomes. The ideas and thoughts of Babylon blended in with the children of Israel right before revival broke out in the land. It is symbolic of an attempt by the enemy to plant illegitimacy among a people to hinder what God was getting ready to birth in the earth. Tel-Charsha means "mound of a craftsman," which was a city in Babylon. (Biblehub.com) The people of Tel-Charsha were skilled engravers, artificers, craftsmen, and carpenters. They knew how to create and build just like the children of Israel. God wanted these people exposed because someone knowing how to do something doesn't mean that the spirit operating behind the work is legit.

Whether or not someone can create and build should never be the total focus, but what kind of spirit does the builder have? Are their hands clean and hearts pure? People can be so mesmerized by people's gifts, talents, and abilities that they don't discern their character. David was a man after God's own heart who was legit, but even though he was a true man of God, he couldn't build the temple. Solomon, his son, built it because David had shed blood. Those who carry the illegitimacy hide behind gifts but carry no grace. Cherub was a place in Babylon, which in Hebrew is the word "kerub," which probably refers to an order of angelic beings. (Biblehub.com) This is probably the most dangerous of those that blended with the children of Israel because this is a false spirit that hides behind an idea of truth. God used Cherubims, who are angelic beings, to perform His work in the earth and who dwelled at the throne of God. 2 Corinthians 11:14 (KJV) says, *"And no marvel; for Satan himself is transformed into an angel of light."* Satan conceals his darkness by presenting enough light to deceive and complete an assignment. Therefore, it's important to be prayerful before connecting your life to anything because you may be joining yourself to total darkness hiding behind an appearance of light. The body of Christ must protect itself from the spirit of illegitimacy and the false. False encounters, experiences, words, doctrines, and powers. Unconfronted falsities eventually become accepted truth. "Adon" means "powerful" and "lord" and was a place in Babylon. (Biblehub.com) This spirit of illegitimacy is a powerful spirit that functions in ruling and owning. When this spirit comes on the scene, it starts off attempting to blend in, but its agenda is to take over. Those who came from Adon were accustomed to control and dominance. You must expose an illegitimate spirit because eventually, it takes over your life and begins to control and dictate every decision that you make. If this spirit is operating in the church and among God's people, it automatically turns people away from God because nothing supersedes the Word of God.

Immer was a place in Babylon and is derived from the Hebrew word "amar," which means to utter or say. (Biblehub.com) The spirit of illegitimacy has a voice and speaks though it is not authorized. God exposes this spirit because if a voice with this spirit gets close to people, eventually, what that voice releases will become the faith of those exposed to it. Those from Immer that blended with the Children of Israel were people who spoke. God shows us a powerful paradigm that we must divorce ourselves from worldly conversations of any sort. It's easy to speak what the world says because believers are in the world. However, because believers are not of the world, they speak what the Lord is saying despite what they see. That becomes hard to do when a spirit of illegitimacy blends itself in with believers and amongst the church. Once you allow what or who is not authorized by God to come into your life, you authorize it to operate. Ephesians 4:27 (KJV) says, *"Neither give place to the devil."* If one doesn't give place to the devil, then the devil has no room to move, maneuver, or operate in that person's life. The individuals that came from Babylon that blended in with the children of Israel couldn't show proof that their father's house or descendants were from Israel. Illegitimacy can't prove that it belongs where it is, but that won't stop it from trying. Emerging Nehemiahs have an assignment in the earth to evict the spirit of illegitimacy from the church, the Body of Christ, and bring purity where the spirit of illegitimacy has embedded itself. God, in this era, is separating the wheat from the tares according to the parable that Jesus told in Matthew 13:24-30. The tare is the illegitimate, and the wheat is the legitimate.

The sons of Habaiah, Koz, and Barzillai were priests who were inserted into the priestly office illegally. They weren't descendants of Aaron. They received a title with no transfiguration. They carried a name that didn't match their spiritual nature. They had a mantra but no mantle. They were illegally occupying an office, therefore, making them illegitimate. The spirit of illegitimacy has crept through the ranks of leadership in the house of God, but the Lord is raising up the legitimate to expose the illegitimate. He's raising up those who will implement in the earth what has already been declared from the heavens. These were excluded from the priesthood as defiled. Jesus in Matthew 15:11 (NLT) says, *"It's not what goes into your mouth that defiles you; you are defiled by the words that come out of your mouth."* Speaking without being authorized to speak defiles one and desecrates the office that they are occupying. A person left to operate with and in defilement will eventually desecrate the place and office that they are occupying. Matthew 15:12 (NLT) says, *"Jesus replied, "Every plant not planted by my heavenly Father will be uprooted."* God eventually uproots those out of places and positions who He has not planted there.

King David's son Absalom carried the spirit of illegitimacy, and his life is a perfect example of how illegitimacy operates and how defilement leads to desecration. Absalom stood at the gate, and whenever people would come to the King regarding a legal matter, he would stop them and validate their claims. He eventually stole the hearts of the people. Absalom was defiled by what was coming out of his mouth. He was illegitimately speaking on matters in an area that he didn't have authority or jurisdiction to function in.

Absalom eventually, through fear, ran his father out of his Kingdom and took the throne as the King of Israel illegitimately. Illegitimate people will always try to terrorize legitimate people out of their assignment. Therefore, one of the spirits that are connected to the spirit of illegitimacy is the spirit of terrorism. Dictionary.com defines terrorism as intimidation or coercion by instilling fear. The spirit of terrorism is a spirit that attacks to further an agenda by instilling fear. Long before Absalom got to the point of running his father out of his Kingdom, we see his attempt to terrorize Joab by continuing to call him so that he could bring him back into his father's presence. When Joab didn't respond in the manner Absalom thought that he should've replied, he burned Joab's field. He was using a terrorism tactic to get Joab's attention. After Absalom took the throne as the King of Israel, he desecrated the office with the many unrighteous things he did while illegally occupying it.

Pride

Connected to the spirit of illegitimacy is pride. Absalom said *"if I was king."* Pride causes the illegitimate to want what people who are legit have and to believe that they can function in and handle what people who are legit function in.

Flattery

Individuals who carry the spirit of illegitimacy use flattery as a tactic to fulfill their agenda and gain a following easily by telling people what they want to hear instead of what they need to hear. Merriam-Webster defines "flatter" as to encourage or gratify, especially with the assurance that something is right. Absalom did this by telling everyone that came to the King regarding their legal matter that they were correct and their claim was valid, whether they were right or wrong. Isaiah 5:20 (KJV) says, *"Woe unto them that call evil good and good evil; that put darkness for light, and light for darkness; that put bitter for sweet, and sweet for bitter!"* This is what Absalom did, and his life immediately became in danger once this became his function. Dictionary.com defines "flatter" as to represent favorably or gratify by falsification. Absalom gratified the people in Israel through false words, and this made it easy for him to steal the hearts of the people. People who don't want to be challenged or corrected are attracted to the voice of people who carry this spirit. Illegitimacy lacks standards. The Bible, in 1 Timothy 4:1, speaks of *"in the last days some shall depart from the faith, giving heed to seducing spirits, and doctrines of devils."* Absalom seduced the people by eventually persuading them to be disloyal to King David. His standing at the gate and saying something other than what the king might've said represented a type of new doctrine of the devil arising. This is one of the reasons why the body of Christ must pray and ask the Holy Spirit to expose who is subtle and not sound.

The devil is not intimidated by people who carry this spirit and won't fight against them because he knows they can't fight against him and be victorious. Another example would be the sons of Sceva, who carried an illegitimate spirit. The spirit that was in them was no match for the demonic spirit that was in the man. People who carry the spirit of illegitimacy don't attract warfare unless they target the Kingdom of darkness, which also may open the door to deception. One who carries the spirit of illegitimacy may assume or perceive that less warfare means more protection and covering from the Lord and heaven when less warfare, in this case, actually means that one is less of a threat to the Kingdom of darkness.

Nehemiah had to be bold to take on this task of checking the records and then exposing and rebuking. He had to have a determination not to be a people pleaser. I'm pretty sure that as he was checking records, exposing, and rebuking, he gained a reputation as harsh. Nehemiah had to be content with not being liked. Emerging Nehemiahs are bold prophets who will obey the Lord by standing up and taking on tasks that will cause them to gain a reputation as harsh.

The children of Habaiah, Koz, and Barzillai were then told that they could not eat the most holy things. The most holy things were food reserved for Aaron and the males of the children of Aaron. It represents a benefit and privilege for one who is in a certain office. Most holy foods were sacrificed to the Lord on the altar. Their benefits were stripped away from them until a priest could consult God with the "Urim" and "Thummim." (Bolinger, 2020) Urim is defined as light. The beginning of the word "urim" is "ur" which means a flame or light. Thummim is the same as the word "tom," which means completeness and integrity. (Biblehub.com) The Urim and Thummim were elements worn on the hoshen, by the breastplate worn by the High priest attached to the ephod (Exodus 28:30 & Leviticus 8:8). In Exodus 28:30, the Urim and Thummim was to be over Aaron's heart whenever he entered the presence of the Lord. It signified that he would bear the means of making decisions for the Israelites over his heart before the Lord. Nehemiah understood that a decision needed to be made and knew the order of how to execute it. When man affirms in the earth what heaven has confirmed, it is by divine revelation. In Acts 13:2 (KJV), The Holy Spirit spoke to the church of Acts and told them to *"set aside Paul and Barnabas for the work whereunto I have called them to."* The high priests who consulted God with the Urim and Thummim were those who possessed integrity and were given revelation from God concerning what direction they should go in a matter. If God by revelation speaks to pure vessels to release others into destiny. He will give revelation to pure vessels to release others from offices and positions that they aren't qualified for. Vessels that carry the Urim and Thummim are once again arising and emerging. Those who are qualified to make decisions in the earth because of their authority are arising.

What Judgment Against Blending Looks Like

Nehemiah 13:23-25 (KJV) – "²³ In those days also saw I Jews that had married wives of Ashdod, of Ammon, and of Moab.²⁴ And their children spake half in the speech of Ashdod, and could not speak in the Jews' language, but according to the language of each people. ²⁵ And I contended with them, and cursed them, and smote certain of them, and plucked off their hair, and made them swear by God, saying, Ye shall not give your daughters unto their sons, nor take their daughters unto your sons, or for yourselves."

Nehemiah saw that some of the Jews had married foreign wives, which Moses had given a commandment against doing. As a result, the children of these individuals that married foreign wives couldn't speak in the Jews' language. This is a representation of a new generation that has engaged in new and strange conversation and doctrine in the house of God. 2 Timothy 4:3 (KJV), *"For the time will come when they will not endure sound doctrine; but after their own lusts shall they heap to themselves teachers, having itching ears."* There are conversations being had now that are seducing because they introduce false ideas, concepts, principles, and hope. This is leading people astray, because if it's popular and fits the culture, it's accepted. There is also a doctrine being preached now that is so far from the truth. However, God is causing His seasoned apostles and apostolic voices to confront and bring order in this area. For those who refuse to repent, we will see the Lord begin to judge them. In Nehemiah 13:25, Nehemiah did five things that we will see the Lord begin to do in the earth and through His apostles, who He's sent to confront and bring order. First, he contended with them, which means Nehemiah confronted and rebuked them. We will begin to see great rebuke again from the seasoned apostles and apostolic voices, both publicly and privately. Secondly, he cursed them, which deals with excommunication. We will see God remove those from positions of authority who have desecrated sacred offices with falsehood. Thirdly, he smote certain of them, which deals with judgment. We will begin to see the Lord bring judgment on those who have intentionally led His people astray by spewing what is false. Fourthly, Nehemiah plucked off their hair, which deals with someone being publicly humiliated and being recognized as a public disgrace. We will see the Lord expose those whose motives are not and have not been pure, whose hands are not clean, and whose hearts are not right. The days of hiding are over, and the days of exposing have come. Fifth, and lastly, Nehemiah made them swear by God, saying, "Ye shall not give your daughters unto their sons, nor take their daughters unto your sons, or for yourselves." This means that the Lord, in His mercy and love, will give those who are engaging and have been engaged in falsehood the opportunity to repent and turn back to Him. The Lord may not perform these in the order typed but will nonetheless see everything in Nehemiah 13:25 come to pass.

The reason why the Lord will judge blending is because it contaminates. The tragedy in and of blending is that the contaminators aren't affected by it; only the compromised are. Their children spoke half in the speech of Ashdod and couldn't speak in the Jews' language. Why couldn't their children, who were the seed of blending, just speak in the language of the Jews and not in the speech of the Ashdod? It was because the compromised became contaminated.

The Dangerous Mentality

Nehemiah 3:5 – "And next unto them the Tekoites repaired; but their nobles put not their necks to the work of their Lord."

One of the most dangerous mentalities that a believer can have is when one thinks that they are above serving. The Tekoites were from Tekoa, a city in Judah. Tekoa originates from the Hebrew word "taqa," and it means "to release a sound". (Biblehub.com) Therefore, the Tekoites were people who created and released sounds. They were also people that had a spirit of entitlement, I believe, because they were people who released sounds. Despite them seeing the need of their community, they refused to serve in building the wall but were content with benefiting from it. There are those who, because God is using them at the forefront of ministry, start feeling that they are above serving. The higher God takes one, the lower they bow in humility, meaning they must keep God and His work as the priority. When one stays low in humility, then pride, arrogance, entitlement, or no other spirits will have a door to grip them because they know that they are who they are by the grace of God. One shouldn't preach in the pulpit if they think they are above cleaning the church's restrooms. One shouldn't lead out praise and worship but then refuse to be an usher at that same church when not singing. Never feel that you are so anointed that you have arrived at a place in God where you're above serving. That's never the case. Jesus said in Matthew 20:28 (NLT), *"For even the Son of Man came not to be served but to serve others and to give his life as a ransom for many."* Jesus came to serve, and then He gave Himself as a ransom for many. Jesus giving Himself as a ransom sums up serving. You give yourself, your time, talents, and treasure for the sake of others. Jesus also said in Matthew 23:11 (NLT*), "The greatest among you must be a servant."* Therefore, you disassociate yourself from greatness when you distance yourself from serving. Your community, church, and the current culture needs your contribution. To see a need and have the ability and resources to assist but refuse to help is selfish. In Luke 16:19-31, there was a rich man who had more than enough resources to help and serve a poor beggar named Lazarus but refused to, and when the rich man died, he went to hell. This is how dangerous selfishness and the mentality of a refusal to serve is.

Apostle Dannie Williams once said while teaching that, "We must move from a rewards mindset to a responsibility mindset." I once heard a Pastor say while preaching that when people desire to join the church that he pastors, they want to set up an interview with him to ask him, "What does this church have to offer them?" His response was to them, "What do you have to offer this church?" To automatically focus on what you can get from what you are a part of and how it can be beneficial to you is called feeling entitled.

Emerging Nehemiahs will be confronted with this kind of culture in their endeavors to build and serve. God will use them to confront those who possess the spirit of entitlement and dismantle the assignment of the spirit of entitlement through the power of the Holy Spirit.

Sensitivity

You won't find in scripture where the Bible says, "And the Lord spoke to Nehemiah," "And the Lord appeared to Nehemiah," or "And the Lord showed Nehemiah." This was not to highlight Nehemiah being inept at hearing the voice of God because he wasn't. This was to highlight Nehemiah's sensitivity to God. While the Bible doesn't record Nehemiah hearing God speak to him, it does record twice that "God put it in his heart" (Nehemiah 2:12 & 7:5). This is a type of a New Testament believer being led by the Spirit of God, whether consciously or unconsciously. In Nehemiah's case, he was consciously led. He was under the old covenant and wasn't saved; therefore, his spirit was not alive to God, and the Spirit of God didn't dwell in him. However, he was still so sensitive to God that he knew when God was giving him the unction to do something. For the believer under the new covenant, 1 Peter 3:4 (KJV) says, *"But let it be the hidden man of the heart, in that which is not corruptible, even the ornament of a meek and quiet spirit, which is in the sight of God of great price."* There is a man that is hidden, this is the spirit of a man and is the real him. This man is called the hidden man of the heart. 2 Corinthians 4:16 (KJV) says, *"For which cause we faint not; but though our outward man perish, yet the inward man is renewed day by day."* What the Apostle

Paul says ties into what the Apostle Peter said in 1 Peter 3:4, *"let it be the hidden man of the heart."* The hidden man is the inward man, the real man who is hidden. Proverbs 20:27 (KJV) says, *"The spirit of man is the candle of the Lord, searching all the inward parts of the belly."* God contacts and communicates with man through their heart, which is their spirit. Emerging Nehemiahs will be sensitive to the Holy Spirit and the witness that He will give to their spirits to make decisions. Sometimes believers make the mistake of waiting for God to speak to them in some grand way. He just may, by a simple inward witness, communicate with man. In 1 Kings 19, God was not in the wind, earthquake, or fire but in the still small voice. Nehemiah's life is an example as to how believers should live, sensitive to God's leading and unction.

The Bible also records Nehemiah praying 9 times, especially in critical moments (Nehemiah 1:4-11, 2:4, 4:4-5, 5:19, 6:9, 6:14, 13:14, 13:22, and 13:29). This means that Nehemiah had a prayer life of consistency. Nehemiah stood in the counsel of the Lord and prayed about everything. Emerging Nehemiahs must have and maintain their prayer lives, as that time with the Father will cause them to be sensitive to the Holy Spirit. When the Holy Spirit gives them a witness in their spirit, they'll be sensitive enough to follow it. Sensitivity to the Holy

Spirit, not just in ministry but in one's personal life, can save your life. You may be driving down the road, and the Holy Spirit speaks or gives you an inward witness to turn left at the next street. Being sensitive and then obedient in a moment like that is imperative. He may be telling you to turn left because if you keep straight past the next street, you may get in an accident 20 seconds later. The Holy Spirit knows the future and will lead us away from danger. In my walk with the Lord and being intimate with the Holy Spirit, my spirit has become sensitive to him, who lives in my spirit. This has come through spending time in prayer with God, fasting, and worshiping Him in my private time and in public worship. Also waiting before the Lord and listening to hear what the Holy Spirit would say and reveal to me. Too, and most importantly, trusting the work, ministry, and presence of the Holy Spirit. This is important because just like Jesus couldn't move where there was unbelief, neither can the Holy Spirit. Jesus said that the believer knows the Holy Spirit (John 14:17), but just because you know someone doesn't mean you can't get to know them better. The Holy Spirit doesn't dwell in the believer just to be there but wants to move in, and for us to know Him in a greater way as we cultivate a relationship with Him. The Holy Spirit is the best friend that a believer has. When you give the Holy Spirit a seat in your life with unlimited access, He draws closer to you, and as He draws closer to you, your focus on Him will cause you to be more sensitive to Him.

Who's Guarding The Gates?

Nehemiah 11:19 (KJV) – "Moreover the porters, Akkub, Talmon, and their brethren that kept the gates, were an hundred seventy and two."

People, especially believers, should never cease to give attention to who's guarding gates, from family gates to gates in systems. Who guards a gate will determine a high percentage of what comes into that gate. This is one of the reasons why I believe voting on every level is imperative. One of the greatest ways people open a door to the enemy is by neglecting to watch, with urgency, who is guarding the gates that affect them, whether directly or indirectly. In Nehemiah 11, Akkub, Talmon, and their brethren kept the gates. Akkub in Hebrew means supplanting, crookedness, or lewdness. (Biblehub.com) The spirit of Akkub operating through a person moves in deception, and the ultimate goal is to overthrow systems or a person in a position. This is why we are seeing attempts to overthrow governments and countries invaded in this current era. Talmon means "oppressor" and "violent." (Biblehub.com) I want to put emphasis on the violent part. There is a spirit called Talmon, which is a demonic entity that is currently operating, and I believe is the cause of much violence in the world today.

This spirit is operating in people that are standing at major gates and have released and allowed a spirit of violence into those gates. It can most times be located where great things are happening. Look at when Akkub and Talmon appeared, during the repopulating of Jerusalem, which was a great move that God put in Nehemiah's heart to birth. They were among the many that settled in Jerusalem. This spirit blends in with the masses, I believe, to attack when people least expect it. This is the reason why we are seeing a lot of mass shootings. This is also why chaotic things at family gates are transpiring, such as domestic violence, children killing parents, etc. Not just in families but in society today as a whole. When Talmon's are dethroned and the spirit is dealt with, then violence will be halted. When these two spirits function together, operating through people, you'll see much violent overthrowing through deception, especially in government.

The Forcing Of An Agenda

Nehemiah 13:20 (KJV) – "So the merchants and sellers of all kind of ware lodged without Jerusalem once or twice."

In this contemporary culture, the agenda of the Kingdom of darkness is being forced to discredit God, defile the things of God, and distract God's people. Just like these merchants and all those that sold goods were camped outside of Jerusalem, the enemy has set his agents at every gate in every system to promote and push demonic agendas. These merchants and sellers in Nehemiah 13:20 had no respect for God or the Sabbath day. They were still outside of the gate even after Nehemiah made an announcement to God's people according to the Law of Moses from God that they shouldn't buy or sell on the Sabbath day. However, the reason why the merchants and sellers were selling on the Sabbath day in Jerusalem is because God's people opened the door to it. This opened the door for these worldly people to disrespect God and the Sabbath. How can the church expect to win the world by behaving in ways that are contrary to the Word? This gives the world fuel to further dishonor God and the things of God. The world figures that if God's people themselves dishonor Him, why should we honor

Him? God is calling for those who will defend the Kingdom of God, the things of God, and fight for the faith without compromise.

The merchants and sellers stood at the gate to make sure their agenda flourished by any means necessary. What made their agenda demonic was that what they were doing went against what God had already declared in His Word. Anything that directly goes against or conflicts with what God has declared is demonic. Nehemiah's response to what was transpiring in Jerusalem was that he set the Levites at the gate as watchmen. Gatekeepers that are emerging are so important in this contemporary culture and in this new era of shifting; their roles are so vital. They will be like those whom the Prophet Amos prophesied about in Amos 5:10. Amos 5:10 (KJV), *"They hate him that rebuketh in the gate, and they abhor him that speaketh uprightly."* Nehemiah setting the Levites at the gate exemplifies a powerful paradigm. The Levites weren't just those who sang songs, taught the word of God, and only focused on the spiritual realities. They also were builders and constructors who helped build the temple in the book of Ezra, guards, and judges. These were a tribe of people who were practical about their spirituality. Nehemiah didn't just lay down and let the people camp outside; he was spiritual in setting the Levites and practical in threatening those men away from the wall.

In this new era, there will be an emergence of Levites. Nehemiah told the Levites to cleanse themselves. They had to be prepared for this assignment that they were about to take on. It required another level of dying to self and being cleansed. This assignment for those that are emerging to man the gates must know it will require another level of consecration. The further God takes man, the deeper they must go into His presence and must die to themselves more until when people see them, they don't see them; they see God. These individuals will be effective and on the front line, stopping demonic agendas from getting through the gates. In Exodus 32:25-29, Aaron and the children of Israel rebelled against God and made a golden calf and worshiped it. Only the Levites who didn't worship the golden calf. When Moses made a call to the congregation in Exodus 32:26 to find out who was on the Lord's side, the Levites rallied to him. They heard the clarion call and responded. God is causing those to emerge who not only hear the clarion call from Him concerning what He's saying but will also respond expeditiously. This is what the Levites did to Moses in Exodus 32:26. In December of 2020 during a phone conversation with Apostle Dannie

Williams, he said to me, "The question now is not whether or not God is on our side but whether or not we are on God's side." God is always on our side, loving us and doing everything that He has promised in His Word that He would do. What does it look like when man is on God's side? When a man is on God's side, it means that he loves and obeys God and fights to uphold His standards. In Exodus 32:27, Moses gave the directions to the Levites, saying, *"Each man strap a sword to his side. Go back and forth through the camp from one end to the other, each killing his brother and friend and neighbor."* The Levites obeyed Moses, and after they did in Exodus 32:29 (KJV), Moses told them, *"You have been set apart to the Lord today, for you were against your own sons and brothers, and he has blessed you this day."* This is a type of what Jesus was referring to in Matthew 10:34 when He said He came to bring the sword and to set families against each other. The Levites didn't care who or what they had to kill to protect the Law of God through Moses. The Levites refused to allow demonic agendas to flourish without a response in Exodus 32:25-29. It didn't matter who they had to use their sword to cut and kill. Are you willing to cut anybody from your life, no matter who it is, to protect what God is doing? If your answer is yes, you are ready to stand at the gate. If there's someone or something that will prohibit you from saying yes, there's more dying to yourself that needs to happen because God doesn't want anyone standing in the way of your yes. Do you love God more than anything and or anybody? Understand, that the Levites couldn't consecrate themselves in Exodus 32 until after they had cut off from among them, those who were forcing a demonic agenda. In life, God will absolutely tell you to cut some people off and out of your life because some people stand in the way of your consecration.

During a separate phone call conversation with Apostle Dannie Williams, he identified this as something or someone "Contaminating your consecration." After the Levites cut off from among them, those who were forcing a demonic agenda and would consecrate themselves, God would bless them that day. Perhaps the people around you and your inability to cut off certain relationships are blocking the blessing that God really wants to release to you. I don't believe that it was a coincidence that the Levites emerged in Exodus 32 in this manner. Their hearts were proven, and God knew that He could trust them to stand with Him if they had to stand alone against the culture. Don't just allow the enemy to force his agendas on your children and families. Ungodly agendas are being pushed and forced through different means. This includes but is not limited to what's shown on television, in music, types of clothing, and events transpiring in the world. As Nehemiah threatened violence toward the merchants and those that sold, believers must be violent with their faith at times. Those at the gates ready to fight for the Kingdom of God against ungodly agendas that are being presented. Nehemiah 13:21 (KJV), *"Then I testified against them, and said unto them, Why lodge ye about the wall? if ye do so again, I will lay hands on you. From that time forth came they no more on the sabbath."* Matthew 11:21 (KJV) says, *"And from the days of John the Baptist until now the kingdom of heaven suffereth violence, and the violent take it by force."*

There must be believers who will not allow the enemy to attempt to take territory spiritually or through practical means. Demonic agendas are being forced and presented, and the world is daring the body of Christ to say anything. They're waiting to reply with "Christians are so judgmental." Christians aren't being judgmental when they cry out against ungodliness; they're upholding the standard of God. Christians love what God loves and hate what God hates. This is why the Prophet Amos prophesied in Amos 5:15 (NIV), *"Hate evil, love good; maintain justice in the courts…"* It is imperative that we do these three things because the closer we get to the coming of the Lord, the more we will see demonic agendas being forced, shifting the climate of the culture for the worst.

Some demonic agendas will flourish more than others. Nehemiah reacted to what he saw happening, but the church of the Lord Jesus must be proactive in our responses to demonic agendas being forced in this contemporary culture. The church must be proactive through preaching truth in season and out of season, praying against ungodly agendas prior to possible manifestation into the earth realm. We can also do this by being practical. We become practical by gatekeepers being on guard and not allowing Babylonian's agenda to invade systems and affect the body of Christ directly or indirectly. Babylon is a worldly system that's anti-God. The church can't be intimidated about speaking up for and against what the enemy attempts to force in the name of not wanting to be judgmental. Jesus in Matthew 10:34 (KJV) said, *"Do not think that I came to bring peace on earth. I did not come to bring peace but a sword."* The purpose of the sword that Jesus was bringing was to divide and cut asunder anything that would separate people from Him and the plans and purposes of the Father. This includes demonic agendas that will keep people from God. The Body of Christ must fight! We must do what Nehemiah told the men of Judah in Nehemiah 4:14 (KJV), *to "fight for your brethren, your sons, and your daughters, your wives and your houses."* Generations are on the line! The enemy is attempting to poison and pervert an entire generation of people through demonic agendas. It is important to note what the merchants' and sellers' assignment was and what they were selling in their assignment. They were selling goods. They were selling and bringing items to the gate that seemed to be good. This is how the enemy is presenting and disguising demonic agendas. He's using what sounds, feels, looks, tastes, and appears good but isn't good at all for man. This is one of the reasons why it's important for believers to walk in the Spirit. Walking in the Spirit starves your flesh, and as a result, nothing in you will respond to demonic agendas disguised as blessings. When you walk in the Spirit, you'll also have enough discernment to know when a demonic agenda is being presented.

How was everything that happened throughout the entire chapter of Nehemiah 13 corrected? It was because Nehemiah's function throughout the entire chapter of Nehemiah 13 was as an apostle. He came and brought order where there was dysfunction. God is causing those with apostolic authority to arise and expose and confront cultures in this contemporary culture. Those who are sent with miraculous power will walk in their power and cause great shift. Apostolic authority will be a difference maker in shifting what is transpiring in regions, systems, and at gates. As the merchants came back not just once, they kept coming back, so will demonic agendas. Just because a demonic agenda doesn't flourish in one system, season, or way doesn't mean the enemy isn't going to try to cause it to flourish in another system, season, or way. Once the Levites get on the gates, they must not come off or stop fighting.

The House Of God

Nehemiah 10:39 (KJV) – "For the children of Israel and the children of Levi shall bring the offering of the corn, of the new wine, and the oil, unto the chambers, where are the vessels of the sanctuary, and the priests that minister, and the porters, and the singers: and we will not forsake the house of our God."

After the children of Israel experienced revival and spent time in the word of God, they made a corporate vow that they would not neglect the house of God. They were making a vow that they would do whatever it took to assure that the house of God was not lacking in any area. This included their time, talent, and treasure. When a person genuinely encounters God, and the word of God becomes hidden in their heart, they won't have an issue committing themselves to the house of God. This is one of the reasons why revival is needed, because when people truly encounter God, then they'll be committed to the house of God. However, if people commit to the house of God without experiencing God, eventually they'll become bored because their foundation wasn't solid through firsthand knowledge about God. The benefits of being attentive to the house of God are very rewarding. One of the reasons King David was so blessed was because of his unwavering commitment to the house of his God. I've heard Dr. R. Shaun Ferguson say on numerous occasions that God spoke to him years ago and said, "Shaun, take care of my house, and I'll take care of your house." Nehemiah asked a question in Nehemiah 13:11, "Why is the house of God forsaken?"

Nehemiah 13:11 (KJV) – "Then contended I with the rulers, and said, Why is the house of God forsaken? And I gathered them together, and set them in their place."

The same people who vowed in Nehemiah 10:32-39 what they would give to the house of God and not neglect the house of God were the very people who did so. What caused them to neglect the house of God? What was more important to them than the house and things of God? What grabbed their focus and stole their attention? The body of Christ must always be intentional in praying for focus because the enemy is out to steal it. The Apostle Paul asked the church of Galatia in Galatians 3:1 (KJV), *"Who hath bewitched you?"* Or I would say what has bewitched you for one who will or has neglected the house of God?" It was sin and rebellion against God that caused them to neglect the house of God. We, as the body of Christ, must have the kind of determination that the Apostle Paul had. He was so focused on God and the things of

God that in Romans 8:35 (KJV), he said, *"Who shall separate us from the love of God,"* or I'll say what shall separate us from the love of God. The Apostle Paul then goes on to list, in Romans 8:35-39, the circumstances that wouldn't separate him and the church of Rome from the love of God. The church is the greatest entity in the earth. The Prophet Micah declares in Micah 4:1 that in the last days the church will be proven to be the greatest entity in the earth (excluding marriage). God is never pleased with a casual, lackadaisical, and lethargic attitude and approach to His house.

This kind of approach and attitude at the root is a matter of the heart. The heart of a person is what allows them to be content with the house of God, taking a backseat and being put on the back burner to their personal agendas.

What happened to God's people between Nehemiah 10:32 and Nehemiah 13:11? The same thing that happened to the church at Ephesus in Revelation 2:4 (KJV), when God told them that *"thou hast left thy first love."* When people's hearts are turned away from God, it becomes easy to forsake His house. I have set my affection to the house of my God.

1 Chronicles 29:3 (KJV) – "Moreover, because I have set my affection to the house of my God, I have of mine own proper good, of gold and silver, which I have given to the house of my God, over and above all that I have prepared for the holy house…"

Those who carry the spirit of David will arise in the last days whose affection will be set on the house of God. Not only will these individuals carry the spirit of David, but they will also have a heart like David. David is described in 1 Samuel 13:14 as a man after God's heart. Despite the imperfection of these individuals, their hearts will be after God's heart, and nothing will separate them from the things of God. David was a man that had such an appreciation and excitement for the house of God that he said in Psalms 122:1 (KJV), *"I was glad when they said unto me, Let us go into the house of the LORD."* The word "affection" in Hebrew is "ratash," and it means "to be pleased with, accept favorably, delight, or to find pleasure in". These individuals will delight and find pleasure in the house of God because of their love and appreciation for it and commitment to it. David couldn't build the house of God because he was a warrior who had shed blood. He still, however, gave of his personal wealth to ensure that the temple was built because of his love for God and His house. David, in Psalms 23:6 (KJV), said, *"Surely goodness and mercy shall follow me all the days of my life: and I will dwell in the house of the*

Lord for ever." He had a mentality that because of God's faithfulness to his life that he would forever remain grounded in the house of God. This remnant who carries the spirit of David will be those who serve in the house of God, give to the house of God, and appreciate the house of God. Therefore, allowing one allowing nothing to shake their commitment for the house of God will assure that they won't purposely forsake it. The days are coming when the house of God will be appreciated again for the place of safety and refuge that it is.

The Sabbath

Nehemiah 13:15 - 17 (KJV) – "In those days saw I in Judah some treading wine presses on the sabbath, and bringing in sheaves, and lading asses; as also wine, grapes, and figs, and all manner of burdens, which they brought into Jerusalem on the sabbath day: and I testified against them in the day wherein they sold victuals. 16 There dwelt men of Tyre also therein, which brought fish, and all manner of ware, and sold on the sabbath unto the children of Judah, and in Jerusalem.17 Then I contended with the nobles of Judah, and said unto them, What evil thing is this that ye do, and profane the sabbath day?"

Not only did God's people forsake the house of God, but some from Judah were engaging in a lot of work on the Sabbath day. When one forsakes the house of God, it's because their affection and commitment for the house of God have waned due to their heart. When one profanes the Sabbath, they intentionally desecrate what belongs to God because their heart has been turned away from Him. The Sabbath day was, in biblical times, a day set aside for complete reverence for the Lord in which no work was to be done. They lost sight of God and couldn't even set aside one day for God. While New Testament believers aren't under the law, every believer should have a place in their life reserved strictly for God and honor it. Judah's agenda became a priority at the expense of their integrity. They knew that what they were doing was wrong, but they became content with compromise. The Lord showed me that distractions didn't make Judah sell on the Sabbath day; Judah did what they wanted to do all along when they had an opportunity to do it. Nehemiah seeing and confronting this issue to bring order is symbolic of God Himself, and through using His assigned voices, confronting the hearts of individuals. Some individuals have turned their hearts away from the Lord, and that's why they've divorced themselves from attending corporate worship and from fulfilling their Kingdom assignments. Judah backslid, and the evidence shows in their profaning. The closer we get to the coming of the Lord Jesus, the more we will see believers who haven't grounded themselves in the things of God backslide. Some have already secretly backslid but will now openly show it. Yes, we are living in a time where many events are held on Sundays; this is a part of the kingdom of darkness' agenda. However, those who are grounded in God and serve Him wholeheartedly don't move at opportunities to desecrate what belongs to God. Judah wasn't just profaning the Sabbath; they were doing it openly. They weren't ashamed to openly dishonor God, as discussed in The Forcing of An Agenda chapter. Those who are grounded in the Lord must also be vigilant because what man may deem as God opening many doors may be a trick from the enemy to break the focus of those in the Kingdom of God.

Kingdom Living

The Apostle Paul in 1 Corinthians 4:20 (NLT) said, *"For the Kingdom of God is not just a lot of talk; it is living by God's power."* Nehemiah demonstrated what it means to live by God's power when he came to Judah and Jerusalem to build the wall and economy back up. He didn't show up on the scene, just doing a whole lot of talk. When Nehemiah opened his mouth to share with the people what God had put in his heart, he already had a plan and was ready to execute it. Nehemiah lived by God's power in all that he did, and as a result, he accomplished everything that God put in his heart to do. Understand that when the Apostle Paul said "the Kingdom isn't just a whole lot of talk," he was referring to it not being one-sided because the Kingdom is absolutely a whole lot of talk. This is the same Apostle Paul who said in Romans 10:8 (KJV), *"But what saith it? The word is nigh thee, even in thy mouth, and in thy heart: that is, the word of faith, which we preach."* This is also the same Apostle Paul who said in 2 Corinthians 4:13 (KJV), *"We having the same spirit of faith, according as it is written, I believed, and therefore have I spoken; we also believe, and therefore speak."* And this is the same Apostle Paul who said in Hebrews 10:23 (KJV), *"Let us hold fast the profession of our faith without wavering; (for he is faithful that promised;)."*

The Apostle Paul taught a whole lot about faith confessions and the power of words, but in 2 Corinthians 4:20, he shows a balance and holistically what Kingdom living is and what it looks like. Kingdom living is displaying that God has given you the power. The word "power" in 2 Corinthians 4:20 is the Greek word "dunamis," which means "strength", power, or ability". (Biblehub.com) It is where the English word "dynamite," which means explosives. The only way that this power can fully rest on the inside of a person, according to Acts 1:8, is if they receive the baptism of the Holy Spirit. In the Old Testament, no one was under the new covenant and had the Holy Spirit dwelling in them as New Testament believers have. The Prophet Ezekiel was, however, able to get a taste of the new covenant when he said in Ezekiel 2:2, *"And the spirit entered into me when he spake unto me."* The Holy Spirit came upon individuals to accomplish a work or to stand in an office. Nehemiah was able to build because God's spirit came upon him to build and accomplish the work. If Nehemiah, with a vision, was able to accomplish his task of building the wall in 52 days and be an effective governor for 12 years, so can you. While people in this contemporary culture have a vision and make constant faith confessions for it to manifest but still don't see the manifestation, a question must be raised. "Is the entirety of the Kingdom living being embraced and practiced, or are we just doing a whole lot of talk?"

Emerging Nehemiahs will be those who walk out of the true definition of Kingdom living. They will be people of results because they don't just spend all their time talking. The favor of God will rest upon them, and as He does, it will not be just a cliche or term that is thrown out so loosely. The Apostle Paul in 1 Corinthians 15:10 (NLT) said, "But whatever I am now, it is all because God poured out his special favor on me—and not without results." There were results in the life of the Apostle Paul because of the favor that he knew was on his life from God. We are entering into the days where favor will be more than just a word that's used; it will be a weapon that's used. No devil in hell can stop the favor of God from showing up in a person's life. Kingdom living and function will be the key to God's best life in the days to come.

The Apostle Paul attested to being accused by others of having a good talk, but his talk not matching who he really was or what he was capable of doing. 2 Corinthians 10:10 (NLT) says, *"For some say, 'Paul's letters are demanding and forceful, but in person he is weak, and his speeches are worthless!'"* The Apostle Paul didn't become offended at these accusations. When you know who you are, you won't become offended with people who doubt who you are. His response to the church of Corinthians was that these people will one day see that what he talks about, he can produce, and show evidence of it. 2 Corinthians 10:11 (NLT), *"Those people should realize that our actions when we arrive in person will be as forceful as what we say in our letters from far away."* Don't walk around in life with a chip on your shoulder, trying to prove yourself to people who don't believe that you are who you know and say that you are. Having this attitude in life and ministry will cause one to exhaust a lot of unnecessary effort. It will also open a door for the spirit of offense, rejection, and pride to come in. In the Kingdom, believers respond with evidence. Let others evaluate the evidence of what God does through you instead of you evaluating what people are saying. When you know that with God on your side, there will be evidence to what you are saying. The Prophet Elijah said in 1 Kings 18:24 (KJV) when there was a confrontation between him and the prophets of Baal on Mount Carmel, *"And call ye on the name of your gods, and I will call on the name of the LORD: and the God that answereth by fire, let him be God. And all the people answered and said, It is well spoken."* This is because the Prophet Elijah knew he had nothing to prove. The evidence of his authority would eventually be revealed.

Functioning & Prospering In An Unfamiliar Place

Nehemiah 11:1-2 (KJV) – "¹ And the rulers of the people dwelt at Jerusalem: the rest of the people also cast lots, to bring one of ten to dwell in Jerusalem the holy city, and nine parts to dwell in other cities. ² And the people blessed all the men, that willingly offered themselves to dwell at Jerusalem."

These men in Nehemiah 11:1 were hand-picked by God because there are no coincidences in God or in the Kingdom of God. As a result of them being picked, they were moved out of their comfort zone and away from what was familiar. At this point they could then be instruments of the plans and purposes of God for what He wanted to do in Jerusalem, and to then for them to receive a blessing. Notice that the blessing wasn't released on them until after they had moved from their towns to Jerusalem. Most times, if not all times, the place where God positions His people to receive His best is outside of their comfort zone and requires them to walk through or function in an unfamiliar place. These men that were moved from their towns could have resisted what was ordained for them to step into at that moment because it meant that they had to leave their homes and everything that was familiar and common to them. Abram was in this place when God told him in

Genesis 12:1 (NKJV), *"Get out of your country, From your family And from your father's house, To a land that I will show you."* We would not know of Abraham in the way we know of him if he had not stepped away from what was familiar to receive what God had for him. God will never allow a man to obey and follow Him and then not reward them. One day in Mark chapter 10, Peter, speaking for himself and the other 11 apostles, said to Jesus, *"We have left everything to follow you."* Jesus then responds in Mark 10:29-30 (KJV), *"And Jesus answered and said, Verily I say unto you, There is no man that hath left house, or brethren, or sisters, or father, or mother, or wife, or children, or lands, for my sake, and the gospel's, 30 But he shall receive an hundredfold now in this time, houses, and brethren, and sisters, and mothers, and children, and lands, with persecutions; and in the world to come eternal life."* The blessing came after their obedience because God doesn't want us following Him to be predicated on what we can get from Him, even though that's a part of it. Our focus should be on the reality that we are being used by God. It is a rich and rewarding feeling to know that God is using you and allowing you to be a part of what He's doing in the earth because God does not use everyone.

Some people will never be able to come into the life that God wants to bring them into because of where they currently are and what they have. Jesus, in Luke 18, told the rich young ruler to sell all his possessions and give his money to the poor; then he would have treasure in heaven. Jesus was trying to guide him into life (Zoe—which is the God kind of life), which he never had. It would have caused him to live a life that he never lived. Jesus told him that after he did what He told him, that he could then come and follow Him and have the life that Jesus was trying to guide him into. The rich young ruler, however, walked off sorrowfully after Jesus told him that he would have to leave the life that he had and give up what he had to get what Jesus was trying to bring him into. The rich young ruler couldn't see past where he currently was and what he currently had. That stopped him from following Jesus. It hindered him from receiving God's best for his life. The place that Jesus was trying to bring him into was unfamiliar to him and confronted what was comfortable to him. Therefore, he decided not to yield to what Jesus was trying to lead him into. What a tragedy! The rich young ruler was in a moment where he was one decision away from making the best decision of his life that would've shifted his entire life. What the rich young ruler didn't understand is that, as in the Kingdom of God, we gain by losing. Prophet Vince Williams once said, "After God subtracts, He adds and multiplies."

Your best life could be in a place that is unfamiliar and uncomfortable in the beginning. Afterwards, however, you'll thank God for doing your life a favor and bringing you where you wouldn't have known to go on your own. The rich young ruler was interested in the path of least resistance. A path of least resistance is a path of known ease, comfort, and familiarity. Apostle Dannie Williams, as a seasoned apostle who has poured into and watched my life, challenged me one day by telling me something I knew but not to its greatest extent. He said to me that "I tend to take the path of least resistance." I'm someone who loves to travel around the world. I love being in airports, flying on airplanes, and taking cruises. Therefore, when things get uncomfortable and seem unfamiliar to me, I know I can get on an airplane or a cruise ship to feel at ease. That's fine if I don't want to have any interest in purpose. A part of purpose and reaching places that God has ordained for us to reach requires taking a path that has much resistance, is unfamiliar, and will make you feel uncomfortable. The rich young ruler's focus was his possessions. Jesus' focus was purpose. Don't miss purpose by focusing on possessions because when one is functioning in purpose, possessions will come. Your best life is a place that is beyond what you can see naturally, but spiritually, you know that you'll get to it. God doesn't want us to get to the end of our lives and then realize that we fought against momentary subtraction that was simply the prelude to a life of addition and multiplication.

There is a remnant of yielded vessels that will prosper and thrive in unfamiliar and uncomfortable places that God has them because of their willingness to say yes to Him. These men were blessed after making the decision to move to Jerusalem. What was that blessing? It was a blessing to function and prosper in unfamiliar territory. God will never lead a man to a place, only to then leave him alone to fend for himself. The Bible says that all the men willing offered themselves to live in Jerusalem. This means that they were not only obedient but willing. Sometimes, things don't flow the way God ordained them to flow for a person, not because they weren't obedient, but because they weren't willing internally to be obedient. Isaiah 1:19 (KJV) is very clear when it says, *"If ye be willing and obedient, ye shall eat the good of the land."* These men ate the good of the land or territory in Jerusalem because the blessing was on their lives.

To function and prosper in unfamiliar territory is to thrive in a place or position that naturally one should fail in because of their lack of experience or qualifications. However, because the blessing of the Lord is upon one's life, they not only thrive in that place, but make it look easy.

There is a remnant who are hungry and waiting for moments like what happened to these men in Nehemiah 11:1-2 to happen for them. They're tired of average living and are waiting on that supernatural moment in which God gives them a door that is both an exit and an entrance. An exit out of the place that they're in and an entrance into what they've been praying to step into, serving, and sowing into. This is why obedience is important. More importantly, quick obedience because delayed obedience is total disobedience. What happened to these men didn't happen in a season; it happened in a moment. Missing moments can cost you greatly, and that moment may never come around again in your life. Jerusalem was larger than the towns and cities where these men came from. These men were handpicked by God to come and dwell in Jerusalem. Who knows if it wasn't only because God chose them to be instruments of His plans and purposes in repopulating Jerusalem but because they had outgrown the place where they were. Oftentimes, when a person has outgrown the place where they are but are so comfortable to the point that they refuse to move, God will thrust them out of that place Himself. Stepping into a larger place can be intimidating because of the demand of that place, but God doesn't prematurely place man in a place that they aren't ready for. People only do that to themselves. So, if you see God thrusting you into greater and it's making you uncomfortable, it's because you've outgrown the place where you are.

If You Knew Everything

Nehemiah 2:6 (KJV) – "And the king said unto me, (the queen also sitting by him,) For how long shall thy journey be? and when wilt thou return? So it pleased the king to send me; and I set him a time."

I find it interesting that the king never warned Nehemiah about opposition. The king, who was over a province himself, would have known some of what Nehemiah was going to face while building in a region. Again, the king's relationship with Nehemiah is symbolic of the relationship that God has with His children. I believe the king intentionally didn't provide additional information, as God does not always divulge the details. If one knows all, then there's no need for that person to exercise their faith. Faith is about believing God in the unknown. Knowing every detail about your destiny could do more harm to you than it would help you. Sometimes the less we know, the better. God won't tell you the whole story ahead of time. He'll let you walk through what's necessary and impart the explanation later. What a strange paradox in the Kingdom that while God doesn't allow us to know everything, nothing should catch us off guard. God doesn't tell us everything because then there would be no need for faith, but because off our sensitivity to the Holy Spirit, nothing should catch us by surprise. God will show us what we need to know so that it doesn't catch us by surprise. Just imagine what might have happened if it was suggested to Nehemiah by the king that:

"Nehemiah, I'm sending you into the land of Judah, and you'll have all the provisions and help that you need to build the wall. You'll complete the wall in 52 days, and you'll be a successful governor. However, you'll be opposed by Sanballat, Geshem, and Tobiah, the Moabites, Ammonites, Arabians, and Ashdodites in building the wall. They will conspire to try and kill you. You'll have to put watchmen on the wall to watch for the enemies that may come and attack those in Judah and Jerusalem. Your enemies will also create false narratives about you, attack your character, and attempt to tarnish your image with lies. False prophets will be hired to try and intimidate you, and you'll have to expose them. You'll have to deal with your own leaders practicing economic injustice against the citizens in the land of Judah. You will have to make great sacrifices as governor of the land and love people living in the region you've been sent to. Meanwhile, some of the very people you've been sent to serve have put their allegiance in the person fighting you.

Amid all this transpiring, a nation of people will be looking to you for you to lead them."

Imagine if Nehemiah heard all of that before leaving the palace of Shushan; he may have never gone to the land of Judah because that's a lot to process. Another example would be when God told Moses to send spies to spy out the promised land. What God didn't communicate was that the people that were dwelling in the land would have to be driven out for them to possess it. What caused Nehemiah to overcome the unknown was his faith coupled with his focus. 1 John 5:4 (KJV) says, *"For whatsoever is born of God overcometh the world: and this is the victory that overcometh the world, even our faith."* Faith guarantees your victory, and as a result, you won't be victimized by circumstances.

Dependency

Nehemiah 2:14 (KJV) – "Then I went on to the gate of the fountain, and to the king's pool: but there was no place for the beast that was under me to pass."

The further one goes in life and destiny, the more their dependency must be on the Lord. Mankind as a whole must understand that God doesn't want them to have their faith in anything or anyone other than Him. God wants man to be totally dependent upon Him. Jesus, in John 5:19 (KJV*), said, "Verily, verily, I say unto you, The Son can do nothing of himself, but what he seeth the Father do: for what things soever he doeth, these also doeth the Son likewise."* Jesus was totally dependent upon His Father for everything, though He was who He was and had some earthly resources at His disposal. Nehemiah had ridden the beast that he had from Persia to Judah and Jerusalem. Therefore, it's safe to say that Nehemiah was comfortable with this beast carrying him. It was familiar to him. However, when he came to inspect the fountain gate near the king's pool, there was no place or room for the beast that had carried him as far as it did. This is symbolic of the reality that there is no room for both God and whatever man deems as helpful and useful to him wherever God is. God will allow who or what mankind depends on to fail just so we know where our help comes from and to bring us into greater dependence on Him. In Psalms 121:1-2 (KJV), the Psalmist declared that *"I will lift up mine eyes unto the hills, from whence cometh my help. My help cometh from the Lord, which made heaven and earth."* Nehemiah had to walk the rest of the way without what he had depended on and had to depend on God alone to bring him to where he was going during his inspection of the walls. Believers must depend upon God through the person of the Holy Spirit to lead, guide, direct, comfort, speak, and make happen what needs to happen. Nehemiah could've gotten discouraged and said, "My beast can't fit, so I'm not going to inspect because my beast can't go." No! He instead went on without what had been familiar to him up until that moment on his journey and survived without it. God will allow every man to hit a moment, season, and time in which they are depleted of what they are familiar with and accustomed to. It is in the impossible moments that man sees that with God all things are possible. A great and powerful lesson that everyone must learn in their life is that there's a great possibility that who and what you started with is not what and who you will finish with. In Nehemiah 2:12, Nehemiah had his beast and was riding on it, but by Nehemiah 2:14, the beast couldn't fit where Nehemiah was going. This symbolizes a shift that will take place in everyone's life, and that that individual's response must be a faith response, as Nehemiah responded. He kept going despite the sudden disruption of what was familiar and comfortable. It was a divine disruption. A divine disruption is a divinely orchestrated disruption from God that suddenly happens to serve a greater purpose and/or protect one from what is unseen. When a divine disruption happens, and one doesn't know why, they should lean on the one who knows all, God. One of my favorite Bible verses is Psalms 131:1. It's such a sobering Bible verse and is a perfect response to divine disruptions and not knowing everything.

David in Psalms 131:1 (KJV) said, *"A Song of degrees of David. LORD, my heart is not haughty, nor mine eyes lofty: neither do I exercise myself in great matters, or in things too high for me."* David first alluded to being humbled in his heart and that he doesn't look down on others. He then said, "Neither do I exercise myself in great matters or in things too high for me." David was saying that some things in life were too high for him to understand and out of his control. Think about who David was: the King of Israel, and he was confessing that there were some things that he couldn't understand and that were out of his control. This should be our response to divine disruptions. Understanding that there is some information that only God knows. Man will never know everything. People tend to only look at how disruptions inconvenience and make them feel uncomfortable in a moment. This is because of a lack of understanding that when it's a divine disruption, a momentary inconvenience can save you from traps of the enemy. It will also bring your life into exactly the place God wants it to be. God will divinely disrupt a plan in 2023 that will save you from a trap in 2027. Never despise a divine disruption, but instead thank God for doing your life a favor. Be open to anything changing and anyone being shifted out of your life at any moment. It's not personal; it's purpose. Know that every divine disruption is and was for your good and is working and will work together for your good.

When Nehemiah in Nehemiah 2:12 took men with him as he went out to assess the walls, the men that came with him had to leave their beasts behind, and Nehemiah was the only one riding on a beast. Therefore, these men had nothing to depend on during their journey, but Nehemiah, who was the leader, still had his beast to depend on. What God was getting ready to do in Nehemiah's life and because of the leader that he would be to a nation and generation, required him to lead by example. Therefore, the Lord allowed him not to have anything to depend upon. This was not only for his sake but for the people he was called to serve as well. There's nothing more perplexing than a leader who's not willing to lead by example. God had to make an example out of Nehemiah's life before he presented his life to a nation. You aren't ready for nations if you aren't willing to allow the Lord to make your life an example. If you say that God has called you to the nations, then you are willingly volunteering for God to make an example out of your life for others. Everybody in scripture who did a big task for God became an example that is now a reference for us. When Nehemiah emerged and started leading a nation, his life was a reference to people on the importance and results of depending solely on the Lord. When Nehemiah stepped into the fullness of his purpose, he found that his life was not his own. When you say yes to your purpose, you automatically give God permission to use your life as an example. Just think about why people follow other people! It's because that person has set such an example that others are provoked to follow them. What a leader presents will eventually provoke those who follow that leader.

Nehemiah was riding on a beast, and those who were with him were walking. Nehemiah was comfortable at that moment, and those who were with him were possibly uncomfortable while walking. They could've gotten offended with Nehemiah and accused him of only being concerned with himself. However, this was a part of Nehemiah's development as a leader. Nehemiah had to understand that one of the great qualities of leadership is being able to have commonality with the people. If people feel that you are above them and there's no way they can reach where you are and that you are only concerned about advancing your life, they won't follow you. Once Nehemiah was off his beast and walking like those he was leading, he could relate to them.

Nehemiah found out earlier in chapter 2, in Nehemiah 2:1-3, the importance of why when one is called, God doesn't want their life to be their own but an example.

Nehemiah 2:1-3 (KJV) – "1 And it came to pass in the month Nisan, in the twentieth year of Artaxerxes the king, that wine was before him: and I took up the wine, and gave it unto the king. Now I had not been beforetime sad in his presence. 2 Wherefore the king said unto me, Why is thy countenance sad, seeing thou art not sick? this is nothing else but sorrow of heart. Then I was very sore afraid, 3. And said unto the king, Let the king live for ever: why should not my countenance be sad, when the city, the place of my fathers' sepulchres, lieth waste, and the gates thereof are consumed with fire?"

In Nehemiah 2:1-3, Nehemiah was in a place of dependency upon the Lord to give him favor with the King according to his prayer in chapter 1. Nehemiah hadn't been sad in the presence of the King. I'm sure Nehemiah, like any other human, had moments of discouragement, but he never showed it in the presence of the King. He never allowed who he was called to serve to ever see him in a state that would suggest that he couldn't function normally. Please understand, God doesn't want us to be the person that keeps it all together externally while we die internally. However, He doesn't want us to be a person that allows our emotions to affect our assignment. In ministry, you are called to serve people with problems, and that is not the time to express your problems. Nehemiah didn't allow his emotions to affect his assignment. Those who serve others are called to be Isaiah 53:7-8 examples.

Isaiah 53:7-8 (KJV) – "He was oppressed and He was afflicted, Yet He opened not His mouth; He was led as a lamb to the slaughter, And as a sheep before its shearers is silent, So He opened not His mouth.⁸ He was taken from prison and from judgment, And who will declare His generation? For He was cut off from the land of the living; For the transgressions of My people He was stricken."

Jesus Christ was oppressed and afflicted but didn't open His mouth to share His thoughts. No one considered how being crucified would affect Him, but that didn't stop Him from fulfilling the call to serve. He died to His will so that others whom He was called to serve may live. A question that every individual should ask themselves when in ministry is, "Am I willing to die that others may live?" What if Nehemiah, when he heard the information that he did concerning the Jews who escaped captivity, those that were left in captivity, and concerning Jerusalem, would've said, "I'm not serving the King today," or "I can't serve the King anymore period, because of what's going on in my life"? He would've been divorcing himself from what God wanted to use as a door to deliverance for a people. When you are called by God, and people are assigned to your life, understand that your decisions not only affect you but those that God has assigned to your life. Nehemiah's decision to stay faithful to his assignment as the King's cupbearer caused a nation of people to be delivered and an entire city and economy to change. One of the worst things that one can do when they're feeling discouraged and defeated is to abandon the place that God has designed for them to find their purpose.

Hanani

Every Nehemiah needs a Hanani. Hanani was Nehemiah's brother and is described in Nehemiah 7:2 as a faithful man who feared God above many. He is only mentioned twice in the book of Nehemiah; however, in that, the Bible alludes to his integrity and records his elevation and promotion to have charge over Jerusalem. Both times that Hanani is mentioned in the book of Nehemiah were at crucial and critical times. The first time he was mentioned was in Nehemiah 1, when he reported information to Nehemiah, which provoked Nehemiah to action. The second time he is mentioned is when Nehemiah is delegating responsibility to him before his exit back to Persia. Hanani's name means "God has gratified me" or "God is gracious". (Biblehub.com) "Gratify" is defined by Merriam-webster.com as "to be a source of or give pleasure or satisfaction to". Therefore, when God sends a Hanani into one's life, he is pleasuring and satisfying that person's life. God is being kind and gracious in sending a Hanani into one's life. Though Nehemiah and Hanani were brothers, they didn't become familiar with one another, and purpose was always the priority. The elevation that Hanani received had nothing to do with him being Nehemiah's brother. It has everything to do with his faithfulness to and reverence for God. I don't believe that

Hanani came to the palace in Shushan to Nehemiah not because Nehemiah was his brother but because of purpose and his heart for Judah and Jerusalem. Therefore, long before his elevation, God saw and knew that he had a heart to do what it took to get his community and the people within his community help. He came to Nehemiah not because he was his brother, but because he knew he had the ability to shift the trajectory of what was going on in Judah and Jerusalem. Hanani, knowing and understanding him, and probably at the time he gave Nehemiah this knowledge, recognized in Nehemiah what Nehemiah may not have seen in himself. This is why everybody needs a prophet around them or at least someone who is prophetic. Prophets provoke through their words. Hanani represents a prophetic voice that speaks into the lives of apostolic voices, and eventually, God brings them into a place where he trusts and delegates to them apostolic authority.

It was Hanani's report concerning the Jews that had escaped, those still in captivity, and Jerusalem that first provoked Nehemiah into purpose. Hanani provokes those around him into purpose. They walk in the Ephesians 4:29 (KJV) call, "*Let no corrupt communication proceed out of your mouth, but that which is good to the use of edifying, that it may minister grace unto the hearers.*" Corrupt communication is not only profane words but any words that are not edifying to a person. Hanani traveled from Judah to Shushan to Nehemiah. Everybody needs somebody who will do whatever it takes to push them, pull them, or provoke them into purpose. Hanani came to Nehemiah on purpose. In Hanani's articulation of what was transpiring in Judah and Jerusalem, his reporting was factual but not evil. Another example would be when the twelve spies went to spy out the city that God promised to give them in Numbers chapter thirteen. They all saw the same land and who and what was in it, but ten of the spies brought back an evil report. That evil report was one of doubt and unbelief, and 2 brought back a factual and good report. Caleb had to calm the people and tell them that they were well able to possess the land. Hanani articulated his message like Caleb, but it didn't cause Nehemiah to feel hopeless but provoked him to purpose.

In Nehemiah 7:1-4, Nehemiah was returning to the king at the palace in Shushan and had yielded vessels to whom he could trust and give responsibility to. Apostolic leaders can't do everything by themselves and be everywhere all at the same time. They need people around them of character and integrity to whom they can delegate apostolic responsibility to that will go in their place. Jesus in His flesh and bone body on earth couldn't be everywhere, but He could send His

12 Apostles. Moses had to appoint leaders to handle certain matters that he was handling because his father-in-law, Jethro, told him he would get worn out if he didn't get help with his responsibility to shepherd God's people. Imagine if Jesus had tried to go everywhere he sent His 12 apostles. Imagine how difficult Moses's life and ministry would've been had he not heeded Jethro's counsel to get a team of leaders to assist him. What if Moses would've allowed pride to grip his heart and said, "I can do this all by myself." He would've gotten worn out. Some leaders get burned and worn out because they try to do it all by themselves, be it all themselves, and be everywhere themselves all at the same time. Pride is one of the quickest ways to cause an apostolic leader with a great assignment to get worn out.

The bible says in Psalms 25:14 (KJV), *"The secret of the LORD is with them that fear him; and he will shew them his covenant."* Hanani feared God above many, and God showed him His covenant by establishing him. Hananis are emerging and being established because they fear God will carry the secret of the Lord. They will carry the secrets of the Lord not because of where God is planting them but simply because they fear God. The secret of the Lord will cause them to have supernatural intelligence to lead in the place of their assignment effectively and supernaturally.

Nehemiah also left Hananiah, the ruler of the palace, in charge over Jerusalem alongside Hanani. Emerging Nehemiahs will need and have people who they will delegate over certain matters after they themselves, as an Apostle, have planted and built in that region. Hannaiah means grace, mercy, and gift of the Lord. (Biblehub.com) Hannaiah being put in charge of Jerusalem was very significant for Jerusalem and God's people. God was telling His people that "I'm extending grace and mercy to you but giving you all a gift, which is a person." This is why it's imperative to honor and cherish 5-fold gifts because they themselves are gifts to men. Ephesians 4:8 (KJV) says, *"Wherefore he saith, When he ascended up on high, he led captivity captive, and gave gifts unto men."* Ephesians 4:11 tells of the 5 gifts that He gave the body of Christ and church. Ephesians 4:12 tells the purpose as to why He gave the gifts to the church and the body of Christ. Ephesians 4:13 tells of the results that God intends to manifest for those to whom the 5-fold gifts have been sent. Therefore, as the Lord sends Hannaiahs into governmental systems, He's sending them as a gift, with a purpose, for results. The Lord is raising up and sending Hananiah's into governmental systems through this earth, and when He sends them, it's God's way of telling mankind that He's not just giving the people under that government grace and mercy but sending a gift. Not only does every Nehemiah need a Hanani, but every Hanani needs a Nehemiah. Hanani must've been in awe seeing his brother lead a great work, serve in government, bring order where there was disorder, by God's grace overcome and combat the forces of darkness, and see the good hand of God moving upon his life. Nehemiah was someone that Hanani could look up to. I believe that the law of association was in operation from Nehemiah to Hanani. The law of association says that because I'm associated and connected to you, what happens in you will eventually happen in me. Hanani had 12 years to watch and gleam for his brother Nehemiah. Because of his association with him, at the end of 12 years, when Nehemiah was returning to Shushan, God elevated him. He became just like who he was associated with—being in charge of Jerusalem, the Holy City and capital of Israel, which was not a small task. One had to possess certain qualities and characteristics to be able to stand in such a position. This is why familiarity is dangerous, because who you should see by the spirit, you see by the flesh. When this happens, you miss the grace that's on that person's life that you could be receiving from. Joseph's brothers, after they were reunited with him, benefited from the grace on his life and where God had taken him. They were able to get food in famine and bring their entire family to Goshen, amongst other things, because of their connection to Joseph. Joseph was their little brother, but he became someone that they could look up to.

What To Expect Part 1 (Prophecy)

Nehemiah 12:43 (KJV) – "And on that day they offered great sacrifices, rejoicing because God had given them great joy. The women and children also rejoiced. The sound of rejoicing in Jerusalem could be heard far away."

What God did for His people caused everyone to rejoice in Nehemiah 12:43, women and children included. This scripture has such prophetic significance, especially in mentioning children. Just like in the days of Nehemiah, what is being birthed into the earth is going to catch the attention of many and cause them to rejoice. In this new era, children will recognize the power of God and give glory to God. We are currently living in a time and day where it appears that a generation of youth and young adults are instruments of the plans of the enemy. However, God is still in control. The prayers of the righteous and the covenant that forefathers have made with God will cause generations after them to be protected from being consumed and devoured by the plots and plans of the enemy. These fathers and mothers saw their children rejoice and give God praise over what He had done. They knew that God was so great that they had to praise Him. Not every child will have a desire for sin. There is a generation that God has preserved for His plans and purposes.

Parents in this era will see their children praise and serve God. No matter where those children are and may be currently doing, the greatness of God and His mighty works will get their attention, and they will give glory to God.

What To Expect Part 2 (Prophecy)

Nehemiah 3:12 (KJV) – "And next unto him repaired Shallum the son of Halohesh, the ruler of the half part of Jerusalem, he and his daughters."

Shallum's name in Hebrew means whisper, which means he wasn't one to broadcast aloud what was happening. Shallum was the ruler of the half part of Jerusalem at the time of building. This means he had influence within the region where he was operating and functioning. There, however, was a certain amount of attention because of who he was. Today, Shallum would be considered a forerunner. He had political control within Jerusalem and a heart for women and them being able to work where mostly men were working. The majority of the people working on the wall were men. This was great because the Lord was calling on the men to arise and take their place of authority in the work of building and protecting. In this hour and era, the Lord will raise up Shallums who will be the forerunners to ensuring that women can function in their assignments without hindrance. Remember, Nehemiah was rebuilding a broken culture, society, government, and physical place. Shallum knew what God had put on the inside of women; therefore, he involved his daughters in the great work of building the wall. They will forever be recorded in scripture as having a hand in the building of the wall. The daughters of God are getting ready to show up in male-dominated industries within the seven mountains of influence.

What To Expect Part 3 (Prophecy)

Nehemiah 7:69 (KJV) – "Their camels, four hundred thirty and five…"

This book is being released, according to the Jewish calendar and Hebrew year, in the year 5783. 5700 in Hebrew means "may it be the year of." 80 in Hebrew means "Pey" and deals with the mouth, words, and decrees. 3 in Hebrew is the picture of a camel, which deals with abundance. The Hebrew word for a camel is "gamal" and means "to deal fully or adequately with", which is retribution, repay, or reward. It's not a coincidence that the Bible points out that the children of Israel had 425 camels in Nehemiah 7:69. It was significant of the era and time that they had entered. Isaiah 60:5 (NIV) says, *"Herds of camels will cover your land, young camels of Midian and Ephah. And all from Sheba will come, bearing gold and incense and proclaiming the praise of the LORD."* This is what happened to the children of Israel in the book of Nehemiah: camels filled their land. Midian means a place of covering. Dear reader, don't move from under God's covering. The covering of the Lord is a place that He has designed for you to stay under so that you don't miss what He's doing in your life. The price of moving will be too great because of what God is releasing in 5783, so keep your integrity by any means necessary. "Ephah" means weary. You may be tired from all that you've had to endure, but keep moving forward. God has brought you into a divine time called 5783, and now your camels will arrive. "Sheba" means oath. You must hold on to the promise that God has given you no matter what circumstances may arise. Camels in the Old Testament were used to transport people, wealth, and different items from one place to another. Caravans of camels would travel together loaded with items en route to their intended destination. Genesis 37:25 (KJV) says, *"And they sat down to eat bread: and they lifted up their eyes and looked, and, behold, a company of Ishmeelites came from Gilead with their camels bearing spicery and balm and myrrh, going to carry it down to Egypt."* Not only are your camels coming, but they are coming loaded with blessings, what you've been believing God for, and everything that God has for you. Prophecies spoken over your life that you've followed God's principles to receive will manifest in this year of 5783 because the camels are bringing them. It's important to know that the kind of camel that is being referred to in Isaiah 60:5 is the dromedary camel. According to Wikipedia.org, the etymology of "dromedary" comes from an old French word, "dromedaire," and a late Latin word, "dromedaruis." These two words originated from the Greek word "dromas" or "dromados," which means "running." The dromedary camels are literally referred to as running camels. They move relatively fast and can run up to 40 miles per hour. This means that the camels are also coming at an accelerated pace. The kingdom of darkness in the last days has intensified in its warfare against the Body of Christ. God, in the last days, has shifted His people into acceleration mode because of the times. In the year 5783, you're going to have Genesis 37:25 encounters. You're going to look up, and suddenly, your camels will be in front of you.

Gold in the Bible was an indication of wealth and status. It was also used as currency. The camels that are coming to your house are bringing wealth and causing your status to shift in every area of your life. Incense, which is translated in Hebrew as frankincense that would come from Sheba, was a valuable product of that country. The camels showing forth the praises of the Lord means that their very movement will cause people to give God praise. God's people will praise Him like never before in 5783. According to spana.org, camels can carry up to 900 pounds for up to 25 miles per day. Your blessings are so big that God will have to use a camel to bring them. According to animalia.bio, dromedaries' fur is short and thick, and it protects them from the sun in the daytime and keeps them warm during cold nights. Their long legs with two toes on each of their feet can spread wide to stop them from sinking into sand. They also have large eyes and good sight, and their large slit nostrils give them a good sense of smell and can be closed during dust storms. All these facts allude to the reality that camels are equipped with enough so the circumstances that they encounter can't stop them. The enemy will not be able to stop your camels from arriving at their destination. The only thing that can stop them is ungodly behavior. As of September 2022, in the Gregorian calendar, which is Tishrei in the Jewish calendar, the church of the Lord Jesus Christ has stepped over into the year of the camels. From Tishrei in 5783 until Tishrei in 5784, your camels are coming and will fill your land.

Type Of Christ

Nehemiah is a type of Christ. Nehemiah was moved by the state and condition of a people and came to deliver them. God was moved by the state and condition of mankind in sin and sent Jesus Christ to deliver them. Nehemiah had 3 main people challenging his assignment: Sanballat, Tobiah, and Geshem. Jesus had 3 main groups challenging Him in His assignment: the Scribes, Pharisees, and Sadducees. Nehemiah only had a certain amount of time to complete his assignment before he was to return to the King at the palace at Shushan. Jesus Christ only had a certain amount of time to complete His assignment before He was to go back to the Father in heaven. Nehemiah returned to Jerusalem after leaving and established order again where there was disorder that God used him to bring during his first assignment in Jerusalem. That's why God sent Jesus into the world as the last Adam to bring His people back to the place where the first Adam in the book of Genesis was. Jesus brought order where there was disorder through His death, burial, and resurrection among men who were spiritually dead. Jesus Christ is coming back to earth a second time to:

1. Rapture His church.

1 Corinthians 15:51-54 (KJV), 1 Thessalonians 4:14-17 (KJV)

2. Then return to earth a third time after the pre-tribulation and tribulation periods to win the battle of Armageddon and set up His Kingdom on earth.

Revelation 16:14-16 (KJV), Revelation 19:11-21 (KJV)

References

Harper, D. (2020). *Emerge: Search online etymology dictionary*. Online Etymology Dictionary. Retrieved from https://www.etymonline.com/word/emerge#etymonline_v_5795

Biblehub.com (n.d.). *600. apokathistémi*. Strong's greek: 600. ἀποκαθίστημι (apokathistémi). Retrieved from https://biblehub.com/greek/600.htm

Wikipedia. (2022). *Economy*. Wikipedia. Retrieved from https://en.wikipedia.org/wiki/Economy

Hitchcock, R. (1869). *Nehemiah - Hitchcock's Bible names dictionary online1869*. biblestudytools.com. Retrieved from https://www.biblestudytools.com/dictionaries/hitchcocks-bible-names/nehemiah.html

Biblehub.com (n.d.). *753. architektón*. Strong's Greek: 753. ἀρχιτέκτων (architektón). Retrieved from https://biblehub.com/greek/753.htm

Orr, J. (1915). *Sanballat - International Standard Bible Encyclopedia*. biblestudytools.com. Retrieved from https://www.biblestudytools.com/encyclopedias/isbe/sanballat.html

Bala'a, M. (2021, April 26). *Sanballat: The Archenemy of Nehemiah*. ArmstrongInstitute.org. Retrieved from https://armstronginstitute.org/334-sanballat-the-archenemy-of-nehemiah

Orr, J. (1915). *Geshem - International Standard Bible Encyclopedia*. biblestudytools.com. Retrieved from https://www.biblestudytools.com/encyclopedias/isbe/geshem.html

Orr, J. (1915). *Tobiah - international standard bible encyclopedia*. biblestudytools.com. Retrieved from https://www.biblestudytools.com/encyclopedias/isbe/tobiah.html

Biblehub.com. (n.d.). *Miphkad. Topical bible: Miphkad.* Retrieved from https://biblehub.com/topical/m/miphkad.htm

Biblestudy.org. (n.d.). *Ephraim.* Bible Study. Retrieved from https://www.biblestudy.org/meaning-names/ephraim.html

Biblehub.com. (n.d.). *6743. tsalach.* Strong's Hebrew: 6743. צָלַח (tsalach). Retrieved from https://biblehub.com/hebrew/6743.htm

Biblehub.com. (n.d.). *2508. kathairó.* Strong's greek: 2508. καθαίρω (kathairó). Retrieved from https://biblehub.com/greek/2508.htm

Abarim Publications. (n.d.). *The amazing name jebusite: Meaning and etymology.* Abarim Publications. Retrieved from https://www.abarim-publications.com/Meaning/Jebusite.html

Biblehub.com. (n.d.). *998. binah.* Strong's Hebrew: 998. בִּינָה (binah). Retrieved from https://biblehub.com/hebrew/998.htm

Biblehub.com. (n.d.). *1419. gadol.* Strong's Hebrew: 1419. גָּדוֹל (Gadol). Retrieved from https://biblehub.com/hebrew/1419.htm

Biblehub.com. (n.d.). *652. apostolos.* Strong's greek: 652. ἀπόστολος (Apostolos). Retrieved from https://biblehub.com/greek/652.htm

Biblehub.com. (n.d.). *Evangelist. Topical bible: Evangelist.* Retrieved from https://biblehub.com/topical/e/evangelist.htm

Biblehub.com. (n.d.). *746. arché.* Strong's Greek: 746. ἀρχή (Arché). Retrieved from https://biblehub.com/greek/746.htm

Biblehub.com. (n.d.). *757. archó.* Strong's Greek: 757. ἄρχω (archó). Retrieved from https://biblehub.com/greek/757.htm

Biblehub.com. (n.d.). *1849. exousia.* Strong's greek: 1849. ἐξουσία (exousia). Retrieved from https://biblehub.com/greek/1849.htm

Biblehub.com. (n.d.). *2888. kosmokratór.* Strong's greek: 2888. κοσμοκράτωρ (Kosmokratór). Retrieved from https://biblehub.com/greek/2888.htm

Biblehub.com. (n.d.). *4152. pneumatikos.* Strong's greek: 4152. πνευματικός (pneumatikos). Retrieved from https://biblehub.com/greek/4152.htm

Biblehub.com. (n.d.). *3772. ouranos.* Strong's greek: 3772. οὐρανός (Ouranos). Retrieved from https://biblehub.com/greek/3772.htm

Biblehub.com. (n.d.). *6963. qol.* Strong's Hebrew: 6963. קוֹל (QOL). Retrieved from https://biblehub.com/hebrew/6963.htm

Biblehub.com. (n.d.). *7782. shophar.* Strong's Hebrew: 7782. שׁוֹפָר (shophar). Retrieved from https://biblehub.com/hebrew/7782.htm

Bibletools.org. (n.d.). *Strong's #82: adelos (pronounced ad'-ay-los).* Strongs's #82: Adelos - Greek/Hebrew definitions - bible tools. Retrieved from https://www.bibletools.org/index.cfm/fuseaction/Lexicon.show/ID/G82/adelos.htm

Biblehub.com. (n.d.). *5342. pheró.* Strong's greek: 5342. φέρω (pheró). Retrieved from https://biblehub.com/greek/5342.htm

Biblehub.com. (n.d.). *972. biaios.* Strong's Greek: 972. βίαιος (biaios). Retrieved from https://biblehub.com/greek/972.htm

Biblehub.com. (n.d.). 4157. pnoé. Strong's Greek: 4157. πνοή (pnoé). Retrieved from https://biblehub.com/greek/4157.htm

Biblehub.com. (n.d.). *1027. bronté.* Strong's Greek: 1027. βροντή (Bronté). Retrieved from https://biblehub.com/greek/1027.htm

Biblehub.com. (n.d.). *2980. laleó.* Strong's greek: 2980. λαλέω (laleó). Retrieved from https://biblehub.com/greek/2980.htm

Biblehub.com. (n.d.). *5927. alah.* Strong's Hebrew: 5927. עָלָה (ALAH). Retrieved from https://biblehub.com/hebrew/5927.htm

Biblehub.com. (n.d.). *8081. shemen.* Strong's Hebrew: 8081. שֶׁמֶן (shemen). Retrieved from https://biblehub.com/hebrew/8081.htm

Biblehub.com. (n.d.). *1918. hadas.* Strong's Hebrew: 1918. הֲדַס (Hadas). Retrieved from https://biblehub.com/hebrew/1918.htm

Biblehub.com. (n.d.). *8560. tomer.* Strong's Hebrew: 8560. תֹּמֶר (Tomer). Retrieved from https://biblehub.com/hebrew/8560.htm

Biblehub.com. (n.d.). *8521. Tel Charsha.* Strong's Hebrew: 8521. תֵּל (Tel Charsha). Retrieved from https://biblehub.com/hebrew/8521.htm

Biblehub.com. (n.d.). *3742. kerub.* Strong's Hebrew: 3742. כְּרוּב (KERUB). Retrieved from https://biblehub.com/hebrew/3742.htm

Biblehub.com. (n.d.). *113. adon.* Strong's Hebrew: 113. אָדוֹן (Adon). Retrieved from https://biblehub.com/hebrew/113.htm

Biblehub.com. (n.d.). *559. amar.* Strong's Hebrew: 559. אָמַר (Amar). Retrieved from https://biblehub.com/hebrew/559.htm

Bolinger, H. (2020, December 8). *What was the meaning and use of urim and Thummim in the Bible?* Christianity.com. Retrieved from https://www.christianity.com/wiki/christian-terms/meaning-and-use-of-urim-and-thummim-in-the-bible.html

Biblehub.com. (n.d.). *8537. tom.* Strong's Hebrew: 8537. תֹּם (Tom). Retrieved from https://biblehub.com/hebrew/8537.htm

Biblehub.com. (n.d.). *8628. taqa.* Strong's Hebrew: 8628. תָּקַע (TAQA). Retrieved from https://biblehub.com/hebrew/8628.htm

Biblehub.com. (n.d.). *Akkub.* Topical bible: Akkub. Retrieved from https://biblehub.com/topical/a/akkub.htm

Biblehub.com. (n.d.). *2929. Talmon.* Strong's hebrew: 2929. טַלְמוֹן (talmon). Retrieved from https://biblehub.com/hebrew/2929.htm

Biblehub.com. (n.d.). *1411. dunamis.* Strong's greek: 1411. δύναμις (Dunamis). Retrieved from https://biblehub.com/greek/1411.htm

Biblehub.com. (n.d.). *Hanani.* Topical bible: Hanani. Retrieved from https://biblehub.com/topical/h/hanani.htm

Biblehub.com. (n.d.). *Hananiah*. Topical bible: Hananiah. Retrieved from https://biblehub.com/topical/h/hananiah.htm

www.ingramcontent.com/pod-product-compliance
Lightning Source LLC
Chambersburg PA
CBHW071300110426
42743CB00042B/1116